Dr. Ély

THE ENGLISH LANDSCAPE

THE
ENGLISH LANDSCAPE

BY
WILLIAM BEACH THOMAS

ILLUSTRATED WITH PHOTOGRAPHS

1938
LONDON
COUNTRY LIFE LTD.
NEW YORK: CHARLES SCRIBNER'S SONS

First Published 1938

PRINTED IN GREAT BRITAIN

PREFACE

I owe a great deal to a great many of those who have written about England and Wales; and to Mr. J. H. Monk-
house for a direct contribution to the chapter on the Pennines; but in general I have tried to reap the harvest of my
own eyes and to give a personal impression of my own
travels among the bye-ways.

CONTENTS

LIST OF ILLUSTRATIONS

The Valley of the Lune at Kirkby Lonsdale *(Will F. Taylor)* *Frontispiece*

INTRODUCTION

The Essence of England

It is a superficial view of the landscape of England to re‐
gard the surface as secondary. It matters supremely, even
in comparison with the rocks beneath it. Geology is the
science of the scenery of the past and the link between past
and present is often slight. The first inhabitants fought be‐
fore they built. They began by destruction, by denudation
of the surface, if the geological phrase may be stolen; and
left much less evidence of the forests they felled than did
those climatic forces which preserved the stumps of prehis‐
toric trees in the Cambridgeshire Fens as under many a
peat hag in the north and west. Our landscape is not
aeons old. It is hardly centuries old. Our historied forbears
made it—village, house, homestead, tree, hedge and crop
matter supremely in inland England (though more in the
south than the north and west) and their differences are
rather a question of variety than species. Cotswold houses
announce the nature of the limestone beneath them. There
is some granite building in Cornwall. Hereford Cathedral
is red with the hue of native strata. Rocks jut out from the
hills here and there, even in the Midlands; and the grass is
shortest and sweetest over the chalk; but bricks and tiles
have travelled widely. Oats and wheat and barley, quick
hedges and cultivated fields, elm and oak and ash, in bat‐
talions or single spies belong to a thousand parishes. Coun‐
ties as wide apart in structure as Shropshire and Kent con‐
fess a similitude due more to the English than to England.

Thus the bright variety of the English landscape is not due most essentially to either astronomy or geology, either to the weather or the rocks. It is due to the home and the homestead that were built therein and the farms and gardens that were gathered about them. England is a homeland in an intensive sense scarcely attributable to 'less happier lands', a double comparative by which Shakespeare, the most English of Englishmen, emphasises his point. The country house is different in kind from the chateau because it is a winter as well as a summer home. Its inhabitants delight in the bare tracery of the trees not less than garden beds and bushes luxuriously upholstered in summer greenery. The parks of the bigger country houses, as indeed of the towns, are peculiarly English. They seem integral to the landscape as to the civilisation. You can travel very few miles without coming into sight of a fringe of trees along the roadway cutting off a wide space of grass freely dotted with others, single trees whose spreading boughs just miss the heads of the grazing stock; and behind them what glorious gardens and antique homes, some contemporary with the older oaks. The English park is the English park whether it is underlaid by chalk or limestone, by green sand or clay, by old red sandstone or what igneous rock you please. Its humblest neighbours in the village are proud of it as a very beautiful English thing. The woods and commons and even the hills and rivers all bear the mark of affectionate human treatment, of places where people have delighted to be. Kipling said of Pevensey that it was fathoms deep in history and often Roman relics overlay relics of an aboriginal folk. Most Roman camps were perhaps old when the

Romans adapted them. And the history below the soil is expressed on the surface, like an old thought in new lettering. The scroll is legible—'God made the country and man made the town', they say. Yes, yes; but the instrument in God's hand when he made the English country was man and woman and child's. It is all fashioned by Saxon and Kelt and Roman and Norman, and their descendants, chiefly their very late descendants. A number of our greatest landscape painters have begun with the home and homestead. Constable was as true as Wordsworth's lark to 'the kindred points of heaven and home': the rainbow and the cart are in touch. They consent to a mutual relation as if they were of the same family. That feeling was indeed a part of the artist's education. The Suffolk master miller used to send the boy out to discover what the wind was doing; and the signals of the wind were the clouds, which the miller's boy used to draw as well as observe. To visitors from our Antipodes the clouds are as English as the landscape; and one of them asked in wonder: do you always have such lovely shapes? After all, the clouds themselves are earthborn, and each country has its own types. Our clouds smack of the Atlantic itself as well as the gentle hills and valleys that direct the upward currents of air and set the wind undulating in two planes—up and down, this way and that.

The gradation of English landscape is consonant with the gradation of the seasons. Our weather is notoriously variable, but it does not vary between extremes. One may say that the rocks and the stars are in agreement to aid the work that the English—for Roman and Norman were soon

'subdued to that they worked in'—have been toiling at these
hundreds of years.

England and Wales have a variety that 'age cannot
wither nor custom stale', but we may recognise the two
parents from which the variety sprang. The west and the
east, however well matched, are sharply contrasted. The
towering peaks and hills of the west coast that comb out the
water gathered by westerly winds from the ocean, have
nursed different makers of scenery, not only formed different
contours. Not even there is landscape a department of
geology. The western people, tending stock on the grassy
fields, have brought into being the homestead in place of
the village. The wall is another thing than the hedgerow,
though its purpose is the same; and the hedgerow, which is
comparatively new, is perhaps as outstanding a mark of our
scenery as the village itself. The homestead is to the west
what the grouped homes are to the east; and both belong to
the landscape only less essentially than the hills and plains,
the woods and rivers, the moors and commons, the chalk
and the granite. Since the scenery of England is in the
hands of the people to-day as in the past, we have a boun-
den duty. It is not preservation, nor even, in Theodore
Roosevelt's phrase, conservation. It is more active, more
formative. England is being remade momentarily like a
rainbow. We must desire to make as well as to keep, to
build fair homes and homesteads, and churches and bridges
and roads, to keep fields fertile and their divisions strong, to
purify rivers and guard their flow to the sea, and to breed a
people who are proud to be the hereditary makers of a land
carved into a homeland by ages of affectionate labour.

CHAPTER I

The Garden of England

Where shall the tale of English scenery begin? In the old, old hills of the west, of Cornwall and Wales, or in the new plains of the east, the fens of East Anglia and the silt land of Boston? In the gentle south or the rugged north? In the track of history and civilisation or along the ages of the hidden stones? It may be allowed to follow the nightingales. These birds, like the greatest number of our visitors, are held to cross the straits at the narrowest points and spread out fanwise, north and west. It may not be quite certain that Albion gets its name from the white cliffs of Dover, but, like the yellow name-boards fixed to a house at the entrance of our villages, they proclaim England to a great part of the world. The sea has cut through the chalk ridge thereabouts very much as the Thames has cut it in the neighbourhood of Pangbourne. Dover and Streatley Hill have a good deal in common. Thus was our insular state determined; and the chalk at Dover has a meaning and a value that hardly belongs to the Boulognais escarpment. It is more true of the south of England than of any Cleopatra that custom cannot stale its infinite variety. Kent, Sussex, Hampshire and still some parts of Surrey, once a most glorious county of down and heath and a dozen other charms—these counties possess a thousand points of beauty that defy analysis: a *catalogue raisonné* of immense proportions

A

Plate 1. Where the Downs meet the sea, Seaford Head

could alone tell the varied tale. Even the types are many: the South Downs, the Hog's Back, Dorking and Leith Hill, the New Forest, the Undercliff and Needles of the Isle of Wight, the plains presented by the sea—at Pevensey, Rye or Dungeness, the crater, so to call it, of the Weald have their own characters. History has influenced the scene hardly less than geography. Caesar and Anselm have marked the contour in rivalry with chalk and clay and green sand. The quick complete changes appeal to the eye of the airman not less than of the walker, who of course is the only real critic of England. You must investigate nooks, you must nuzzle into lanes and spinneys to discover the wealth of the landscape; you can tell only by touch that it is cloth of gold. Yet all who enter England by air to descend at Croydon are ravished by the general view. Here is an epitome indeed! The order has been obeyed:

> *Let the world's riches that dispersed lie*
> *Contract into a span.*

The span is small enough and spacious grandeur is missing, but nothing else. Some few of the things that time has effaced to the eyes of the pedestrian appear to the airman and much more clearly to his camera. An overgrown Roman (or Saxon) road may be only less clear than the ribbon of a shining river. Take Silchester. It was a thriving place. After Caesar landed in the Isle of Thanet he planned his roads and made Silchester the focal point. To-day Silchester is incredibly Englished. It is done into English by time and its chief agent, green grass. You can watch with your eyes the spread of Christianity itself unfolding like the leaves of a chestnut in spring. The leaflets branch from the Pilgrim's Way, whose spiritual bourne was Canterbury. The City still possesses every sort of antique beauty from Cathedral to tithe barn.

It is worth remembrance by the student of English land-scape that from Sturry Court, which has history in every stone of the house and every rafter of the barn and even in the very form of the garden—from this house came forth the first of the 'regional plans' that many preservers hold to be the one means of salvation. For Kent itself, proud in the title of the Garden of England, was to be defaced by the outward and visible signs of a later industrial revolution. Lord Milner, who first realised the threat, once said that in a hard-working life he never faced a harder job of work than persuading some dozen local councils to co-operate in a general plan. How much of the wealth of England lies in coal and how much splendid scenery is made by the strata in which coal is found, but the stuff has the defects of its vir-tues and they become evident when it is brought to the surface. He died before the first of the scenic surveys (a form of literature invented by the Council for the Preserva-tion of Rural England) was planned at his home, Sturry Court.

If Canterbury was the spiritual headquarters of England, Winchester was the political capital, and both towns keep a scenic quality belonging to their antiquity. In both the Cathedral is a scene in itself; and Winchester is a good example of the peculiar charm of English churches de-scribed by Milton in one of the most cunningly compressed bits of description in the language. Its tower is 'high in tufted trees'; and oddly enough, it was founded on trees. Winchester was in part a marsh below the beech forests. The builders in despair of reaching solid ground founded their huge cathedral on what was in essence a raft of un-treated beech-trees. They were as sound as when they were laid some eight hundred years earlier when at last it became necessary to build concrete pillars (by aid of divers) on the solid ground below the swamp.

No single feature of England is so well known about the world as the white cliffs of Dover; and it has companions all along the coast past the Five Sisters up to Beachy Head, which is the true terminus of the South Downs, and if an inquest as to the growth of English landscape begins there, the tale takes on a semblance, a sentiment of continuity. On the chalk downs our ancestors got their heads above water. They escaped from the forests and could more easily make roads, which are the veins and nerves of civilisation in all ages. The story of the English landscape may well begin with the cliffs of Dover and the harbour of Dover; with which Turner played imaginative tricks, without losing the character of the scene. Yet the journey both to the west and the north is strangely interrupted. The white cliffs that rise again by Eastbourne and Beachy Head have wholly van-ished before you come to Rye and Battle and Hastings. Some imagine that a vast river, of South American propor-tions, rising away beyond Ireland, came down to Dover; but let the visions of geologists be; it is enough for the pre-sent that a region of distinctive qualities, quite alien to the chalk, begins and continues northward almost to Seven-oaks, and the approaches to London. It has a name of its

very own. Marsh and fen and wold and down; combe and
dene and pwll, lake and tarn and gill are generic terms.
There is only one Weald or Wield or Wylde, to take some
of the various spellings. To-day it is so little wild that some
of it is known as the Garden of England: for few districts
are so closely and affectionately cultivated. William Cobbett, whose *Rural Rides* is unrivalled, began with the Weald
and knew exactly when he had reached it, wherein he dif-
fers from most people. He was no geologist. He was not
aware that the Weald was an anticline, but no man knew
better what lay immediately below the top spit of soil and
what an influence the subsoil exercised upon the surface
cultivation. He was immediately aware when he left the
chalk and entered the boundaries of the anticline. The
change was announced by the crops, which he found,
severe critic though he was, as nearly perfect as possible.
The Weald perhaps was once uplifted and the stretching of
the surface made weathering a quick and easy process. Soils
quite foreign to the farmer on the North Downs were
reached and left available to the cultivator and indeed the
miner. The so-called Hastings Beds supplied iron. Forest
trees that rejoiced in rich soil and a warm clime played the
part of coal. Yet the Weald, though a very distinctive district, is one of the least uniform in all England and that is to
say much. It is rich with orchards and hop gardens, with
deep grazing and the perfection of arable soil; but it em-
braces Leith Hill which is a thousand feet high and part
of Ashdown. The forest itself, lovely in all its aspects, is a
study in contrasts. Some of the woodland glades suggest the
New Forest. You emerge from them and in the twinkling

of an eye find yourself on a heath that might give a Thomas Hardy the impression of Egdon itself. Heather differing curiously in colour, though of one species, is the chief crop. The southerly view is spacious and splendid, for you stand high above a plain that extends to the sea. If you would know the quick variety of southern England go out from Tunbridge Wells (through which passes the boundary of Sussex and Kent) into the wooded parts of Ashdown and thence on to the heath before dropping to the scoop of the more deeply worn land. The beginning, middle and end of your journey have no sort of likeness to one another; and never suggest that the district in which they are deserves a single, generic name.

It was written several centuries ago: 'There are diversities of opinion touching the true limits of the Weald; some affirming it to begin at one place, some at another . . . it may more reasonably be maintained that there is no Weald than to ascertain where it may begin or end.' Mr. Ernest Straker, who has made a special study of Wealden iron, has found a compromise between the historians and the geologists. He confines the Weald to two types of soil, to Wealden clay and the iron sands of Hastings. It is eloquent of the course of our civilisation that this region should be to-day known for its loveliness and its richness though its old names indicated its terrors. The Anglo-Saxons called it the Wylde, and the Romans, adopting a Keltic word, called it Anderida—the untrodden place.

The varied character of Wealden scenery has been enhanced by the sea, for it runs down to the sea not only at Hastings but at Rye, which is a recent gift of the sea, re-

Plate 2. The Weald of Kent, from Crockham Hill

claimed by nature, with little or no direct human assis-
tance. Romney Marsh is within its circle and there are
glorious haunts of the marsh-loving snipe near Roberts-
bridge, where grows also the cricket willow, besides farms
rich in clover, corn and even forest trees. For the rest the
Weald is pinched between the South Downs running westward from Beachy Head or Eastbourne and the North
Downs running north and east. It is a curious thought
helpful to a perception of the inwardness, so to say, of the
landscape that the Weald strata are of soft water origin representing, some think, an extinct river and lake while
round it as walls are the escarpment of the chalk composed
of the integuments of marine creatures. The clays enclose
the iron sands very much after the pattern of the downs
round about the clay. The inner angle of their junction is
about Horsham. West is the clay and then the chalk; east
are the Hastings Beds. Tenterden is in the eastern angle,
Tunbridge Wells is on the Hastings Beds, Tonbridge just
on the Wealden clay. The Pilgrim's Way makes one boundary line for a space. You may perhaps best appreciate how
the Weald lies and discover many glorious views by looking
south from vantage spots near Sevenoaks, Reigate, Dorking
and indeed Guildford, though that is a little further re-
moved into the chalk. Such views are as well known as any
in the island. Cobbett noted that Kent farmers sent much
of their produce to 'the Wen' (as he called London *ad
nauseam*). It is certain that London in return sends its inhabitants in shoals to Dorking and the Hog's Back. More
and more do the urban crowds follow, though by a different mode of motion, the habit of Cobbett, who travelled

whenever he could from his four acre farm in Kensington to see country that was real country. What a history has the Weald! First a great deep forest, and where not forest, marsh; much later the chief of manufacturing centres, almost a Black Country; then as it became a depressed area, the chief and best of all industries came into possession; and out of the forests, out of the mines, blossomed the Garden of England, a country of gentle undulations, each rise opening new pleasures to the sight, new signs of a rich earth and pleasant clime. It is not surprising that Harold defended his country at Hastings. It is not accident that Canterbury is the heart of the English Church (though Winchester once outrivalled it) and that the Pilgrim's Way seeks the protec-tion of the Weald. It is historically proper that the best of agricultural colleges is at Wye and that Bodiam Castle is neighbour to some of the first great country houses that dis-pensed with fortifications, and the loveliest of old cottages have remained unaltered for six centuries, though their inner beams are made of the despised elm tree, and not of oak.

England grows bigger and not smaller, as many fear, and nowhere does it encroach on the sea as on the south and south-east. Dover, though not a great harbour, is more eminent than ever it was now that the old harbours, now that the other Cinque Ports, are denied to ships. Their busy life has not passed clean away like Silchester's or Avebury's, but they have lost touch with the great world and are the more homely and restful. It is a sign of their new character that the most strongly marked feature of the landscape is a line of contiguous links. The word, after all, is a landscape word meaning sand and dune, though it has travelled far.

Of all the old harbours that have now an inland mood Rye town and its links are the quaintest, though nothing compares with Winchelsea as a single antique gem. The Rye plains are spacious. The little mounted town that looks down on them is a haunt of artists who delight as much in the sails on the quiet river as in the unique quaintness of the houses on the hillock. Sea holly binds the dunes, gorse and grass, and among brighter flowers, viper's bugloss have colonised both pebble and sand. Some of it is now as fit to breed a special race of sheep as Romney Marsh nearby. This breed has the distinction of being the only animal of its sort to appear on a postage stamp! It may be taken as a token of the utter individuality of such morsels of English soil that they have given origin to races of stock which find there their optimum of conditions. Romney Marsh and Southdown sheep belong to their country not less suitably than Welsh mountain sheep or Cheviots or Herefords or Highland cattle to theirs.

Owing perhaps to upheaval of the chalk and later wearing and attrition, iron sands and green sands and London clay are near the surface; and with the chalk produce hills and valleys that have their special growths and have encouraged special cultivations. The covering of the valley clays is chiefly cultivated grass and uncultivated trees, the sands have bred heaths; the chalk in places is so hard that it makes building stone and the Maidstone quarry is big enough to be a feature of the landscape. The soils have encouraged industries. The new Kent coalfields have completely changed the scene and banished the rural air. By way of compensation the old iron factories, founded in the

Hastings Beds, and heated by the Sussex forests, have left traces incredibly small except to those who have peered closely and made study of the days when factories of the Weald and its neighbourhood turned out the iron railings of St. Paul's Cathedral. The use of the wood of these southern counties has had a more continuous history than the iron in the soil. The fine oak woods along the Sussex and Surrey border have a special quality of timber. They supplied the timber out of which Westminster Hall was built. In our day, five hundred years later, when the beams were eaten out by the death-watch beetle, the builders went back for their repairing timber to the same forest, even to the same part of it from which the first beams had been cut. The great trunks used for the repair were perhaps saplings alongside the old trees felled for the first building. So continuous is our physical history.

The Weald, which like Pascal's universe, has its centre everywhere and its circumference nowhere, harbours a great number of quiet and lovely villages: most English, but as different as may be from the more famous villages of the Cotswolds. If they have a parallel it is in the little gem of Ewelme, hidden in a fold of the Oxfordshire chalk. The quality of most of the south-eastern villages is a sort of homely warmth. They are 'wrapt from the world' even when discovered by pilgrims from the new world. One must think first perhaps of Chippingstone, a true Wealden village, and of Alfriston, different though they are, as in the Cotswold, Chipping Campden and Broadway force themselves into prominence. Has nature or art the more to do with the charm? That great walker Hazlitt 'the epicure',

demanded nothing more than a curve in the road. At Chippingstone the curve where the pale of the great country house begins is integral to the beautifully proportioned line of old houses, of the post office and the inn; and to the historic church compact of medieval virtues that fills the elbow corner. There is nothing more English in England, unless it be the scene at the entrance to the hospital on the slope of the hill into Penshurst, which is near by, a perfect example of the many 'hursts' that describe southern villages.

Alfriston has greater claims to prominence by reason both of its history and its architecture, but there the flourish set on its beauty is the view from the hill above it. The wide prospect below most of the higher land has some suggestion of likeness to the view from Bredon and the Malvern hills; but in Worcestershire the features of the landscape below you are more definite and precisely outlined, more like an airplane view. Though in both you may look over orchards and hop fields, which must be like one another, in what-ever country found, the more plentiful forest trees of the south-east 'half reveal and half conceal'. You have always the impression that something yet lovelier is concealed. There is no mosaic pattern. Kent shares in the quality of Sussex. Even the queerly shaped oast-houses are dovetailed into the fringed paddocks.

A supreme example of scenic dovetailing of another sort, very characteristic of Sussex, has lately become a national possession and, very fitly, a school of foresters. Whether you walk or drive you must pass between and among woods to your first glimpse of Gravetye Manor. The character of England centuries ago forced our outdoor artists into taking

Plate 3. The Cuckmere valley in the Sussex Downlands

the lead in landscape gardening. John Evelyn's holly hedge belongs to the scenery of our literature. The revived school of landscape gardening in the nineteenth century had its spiritual home round Mr. Robinson's manor house at Gravetye. Is it possible that a place of such deep quietude could have been built by ironmasters within short reach of their factories? It is now quite close to the most modern of electrified farms—at East Grinstead! The grey Elizabethan house belongs to the scenery, but it is the garden that mat⁄ters most. Its paths and pergolas pass into fields and woods. There is no boundary. The fir wood on the knoll belongs to house and garden not only by juxtaposition but because it was part of the inspiration of the landscape artist. You sa⁄vour there the very essence of inner Sussex, of inner England.

Yet other and sharply contrasted attributes of those coun⁄ties—of Kent, Sussex, Surrey and indeed Hampshire, have been more widely bruited. Everyone knows of Ashdown Forest, of the Hog's Back and of the North and South Downs. Even Rudyard Kipling, the laureate of Sussex, thinks first of Sussex by the sea; the South Downs, more than any other bit of England, inspired the greatest of our writers on landscape, W. H. Hudson. That pioneer in emotional delight in our scenery, Richard Jefferies, who finally fell into sheer mysticism, was born (at Choate) in Wiltshire and greatly inspired by down scenery, though perhaps the most famous passage of imaginative description of a country scene in the language concerns Dorset. The enormous gloom of Thomas Hardy's picture of Egdon Heath has no parallel. Perhaps the quiet pools of peace scattered here, there and everywhere—like Ayot in Herts.,

Hemingford in Huntingdon, Stratford St. Mary in Suffolk, Ewelme in Oxford, Weobley in Hereford, are too complete. 'The green thought in a green shade' is enough without words, too peaceful to suggest words. Only seeing is believing; and you must see at your leisure.

The South Downs from the cliffs of Dover to Beachy Head and the more northerly spur which includes the Hog's Back that looks down on Godalming and Guildford, go near to being a type of scenery, though the prospect never repeats itself. The essence of the downland, where the neat mealy-nosed Southdown sheep are at home, is an uninterrupted ridge clad, thanks partly to the sheep, in soft sweet grass. The clean contour is what matters; and for this reason any building may be aesthetically ruinous, as any building, much more the villa popular at the time, wholly ruins the cliff line in parts of Cornwall—Looe, for example, and of Devon. As you walk the crown of the down —among the sheep, among the innumerable little snails that attract the scuttling wheatears, you may often look down on both sides to trim and homely scenes in sharp contrast with the naked ridge you walk. Nowhere do isolated homesteads look more snug. Often woods largely of beech climb the inland slope to the point where they begin to meet the salted winds. Yews, too, are congenial to the soil and there is no rival to the great group of them above Chichester. It is perhaps its parallelism with the adjacent sea that gives its peculiar distinction to the South Downs, compared with any other chalk upland. They belong to the English Channel, to the silver girdle. They are of a piece with the Dover cliffs.

CHAPTER II

The Downs

When Caesar landed at Woolmer, on the pleasant undulating land on which Woolmer Castle looks
down, he probably blessed the chalk that had met his eyes
as his ship drew near. It gave him an easier advance inland
than the Weald. Though some parts of the chalk downs
were forested, some gave smooth progress, and on chalk uplands, roadways had been built long before his arrival. To
the inhabitants of so deeply a humanised landscape as ours
to-day the nature of the underlying rocks is an after-thought.
A few yards of soil is all that concerns them. The Cornish-
man, of course, is aware of his granite and the Gloucester
villager knows that his house is an advertisement of the
limestone beneath his feet; but neither stone is quite in the
same category as chalk. It is dealt with daily. It comes to the
very surface in every sort of manoeuvre by man or rabbit,
and it descends to a depth beyond all probing.

It matters supremely in southern and eastern England.
Perhaps no geological formation more definitely expresses
itself in the surface of the country, when it comes near the
surface. It may dip down and be overlaid by clay or peat or
gravel or sand or deep humus. Even if it is no more than ten
or twelve feet below the surface, its actual influence on the
country that we see is small. If you walk across a farm in
Hertfordshire you may come upon an occasional chalk-pit

probably overgrown with the wild clematis or old-man's-beard, which is one of the flags indicating chalk. You may notice on the tilth the great number of flints which are the commonest of companions to chalk. The occasional beech trees may be so spacious in the spread of their boughs and so columnar in their trunks that you will infer the presence of chalk about their roots; but the general farmer and others who have made our scenery have paid little regard to the deeper subsoil. The chalk belt that runs from the south coast almost to the north-east coast of England subserves the lowest plain in the island. It almost edges the Fens, which are themselves in parts below sea level. It dives beneath the Wash and rises again for a last appearance in Lincolnshire. We do not regard East Anglia or the district that immediately bounds it on the west as characteristically chalky; for the chalk is well below the plough. Where Hertfordshire, Bedfordshire and Buckinghamshire meet the chalk begins to win and dominates all other influences. It is intolerant of any covering and often where the ridge is high the accumulation of humus is not more than a few inches deep. The rabbits throw out the morsels over the surface and where the ploughs venture they leave a white wake. Ivinghoe Beacon is the crown of the district which is compact of chalk, but there are many rather humbler beacons, such as Whipsnade, where the prison homes of the tigers are cut out of chalk which gives both firm walls and good drainage. Parts of the ridge thereabouts face the south-west and the direction has taken on a new importance, for against these the prevailing wind of our island blows with such regular force that the glider finds his optimum of conditions. The horizontal wind becomes almost vertical as it hits the escarpment and lifts the planes as seagulls are lifted to their nests on west country cliffs.

From the ridge of this grass cliff the view is magnificent, if mild. The plain in which Aylesbury lies spreads out below and the eye can travel into Oxfordshire, even to Oxford itself. All is very green, and populous, for the villages and towns multiply. It is true that some of them have been murdered by want of thought or planning, and by architecture as bad in art as in craft. The pleasant old town of Dunstable just below one splendid bluff of the downs has been virtually joined to Luton, one of the most prosperous towns within England; and economic prosperity is not always correlated with beauty. Its factories are well designed for their purpose and the workmen's houses are free from such structural inadequacy as defaced the industrial revolution; but the town is more remarkable for the avoidance of certain evils than the achievement of any individual beauty. It owed perhaps its origin to the presence of the upper reaches, or sources, of the Lea, the pleasant meandering stream 'that oft doth lose its way', as the poet Spenser noted, before it is straightened out as it nears London and is used to supply its millions with water.

The Chilterns themselves are very dry; and in general one may say of England, in spite of some salient exceptions, that the population varies directly with the water supply. The rule is: the drier, the emptier. Hamlets and houses are rare on the uplands, as on the Wiltshire downs, though they were more frequent, it is held, in the unrecorded days of our Saxon forbears, when the water level was probably a good

Plate 4. A valley in the Chilterns; the Chess at Latimer

deal higher. Water filters through chalk, and the water level rises above the less porous strata below the chalk in prompt obedience to the rainfall. The apparent source of such streams as the Lea, which is a typical example, may climb the slope perceptibly after one wet season.

It is a proper addition to the variety of English scenery that it changes in response not only to the different seasons, but to the nature of each season. The valley of the Lea where it flows down the foothills, so to say, the almost in- visible foothills of the Chilterns, bubbles with springs im- mediately after a period of considerable rainfall. Many of them are used for the growth of watercress. The beds are fed, not as is generally thought, from the stream itself, but from individual springs gushing out at a little distance. The growth of sedge and rush varies surprisingly; and in wetter seasons your riverside walk is forced into wide detours.

On the upper parts of the chalk ridge that we call the Chiltern Hills, the upper valleys, though due doubtless to the action of water, are for the most part dry. The grass is short and sweet and springy, interspersed with a rich but inconspicuous flora. The meadowsweet of the river valleys has been changed almost into an Alpine plant. The un- broken lines which fix the exact pattern of the hill on the eye as persistently as if a few hundred feet of chalk were a towering Matterhorn, can boast a scenic value all their own. The downlanders long for it as a mountaineer for his peaks. It has pleased the authorities of the Whipsnade Zoo to un- turf a piece of the chalk on the slope into the shape of a lion, as it pleased another artist two thousand years ago to depict a horse on the Uffington downs. The possibility of such an ornament is indication enough of the shallowness of the turf that covers the chalk. The slope is bare and its edge unbroken to the view; but when you have topped it from the westerly side, what a change is there, my countrymen! You pass almost at once from bareness to richness, from the shortest grass to towering trees; and the variety, proper to England, is expressed in its highest terms. The beeches prove themselves the greatest of chalk-lovers, but fir and oak and not least the wild cherry flourish abundantly. Some of the minor roads crossing the frontier of Herts. and Bedfordshire or Buckinghamshire are as splendid in their fashion with autumn coloration as the banks of the Danube or Newfoundland plains; and the wild cherry is the crown. Such scenery is no dead thing, nor has it any of the constancy that belongs to much lake and sea and mountain scenery. If it flames in autumn, it is bridal in spring when the cherries are in flower; and there are some countrymen who think it even more beautiful still when you look to a wider view through the filigree of bare boughs. There are several very well-known examples of the sudden rich loveliness into which the gentler slopes of the down break. Ashridge, of which the kernel is now national property, is one; and the area of park-like land is wide. The abundantly timbered slopes and undulations lead to the sharply contrasted common of Berkhamsted in one direction and the naked down in another. It is a place of which the scenic history has been successfully studied and it is characteristic. The original forest was attacked by the early inhabitants and some few hundred acres cleared for husbandry and the building of a hamlet. The folk continued to enlarge the clearing till the community had the use of many hundred acres, some of it good farming land, some waste or common. Then in the eighteenth century came formal enclosure and hedges were planted; but the common remained where still the public at large has the right of 'air and exercise'. The privilege came to have certain limitations. Only the lords of the manor, who are a golf club, have the right to play an organised game. They too, as on other commons, have in some degree influenced the scenery. There is more short sweet grass and less ling and gorse.

If anyone should desire to experience what the Chilterns are, not only in themselves but in their setting, he could scarcely do better than journey from the quaint, pretty little village of Ivinghoe in the plain up the down to the beacon or to Whipsnade and over the ridge by Ashridge and Berkhamsted. The past will whisper in his ear all along the route, while his eyes are filled with a present scene as various as the historic tale. Another famous spot at the edge of the Chilterns is Chequers. It is unique among scenic gems for a psychological reason. The gift to the nation of this most English country house and garden was inspired in the first instance by the imaginative idea that our future prime ministers, to whom in turn the place will belong, would be subdued to their environment: a few days, a week-end, spent in the deep, deep country would help to lend them the serenity that comes best and most surely from the contemplation of nature. They would come within reasonable reach of Andrew Marvell's ideal and

> *Annihilate all that's made*
> *To a green thought in a green shade.*

The setting is as green and peaceful as any place in England and a brief walk takes you within reach of spacious views. The place would convert the most deeply engrooved urban Goth into an ardent preserver of rural England. Such a conversion has been achieved in fact.

In most districts where the ridge is high trees and hedges both are rare enough to give the scene that bareness and distinctness of outline that we associate with the down. Even where the ridge has sunk to a height of three or four hundred feet above sea level and is cut by living streams, such as the Lea and its parallel neighbour the Mimram, water is often not found at less than 150 to 200 feet. The underground lake, so to call it, or the saturation level of the chalk is in many places so consistent that the well-borers know to a foot or two where they will tap it. It bubbles out on the river valley, and will be found just at that level wherever the boring is made. The height above the valley will exactly determine the depth of the well. Yet upon the chalk lies a great variety of soils including clay, gravel and sand. When a survey was taken, for example, of the Welwyn Garden City, which is close to the Lea, all these three were found. The gravel was as sharp and clean as if it had just been washed, the sand was pure and as good brick clay was discovered as you would find at Arlesey or Huntingdon or Peterboro'. Such deposits lying cheek by jowl are a hidden cause of the quick changes in the scenery, of the alternation of grassland and tilth, of oak wood and beech wood, of common and farm. The oaks of immense girth and great antiquity in Hatfield Park bear as true witness to the weight and toughness of the soil as the firs of Sandy's strange hill or

the extent of market gardens on the Bedfordshire plains indicate lightness and dryness in their varying degrees. The
Chilterns may be thought hardly to deserve a special name.
In one respect they are no more than an undistinguished bit
of the great chalk system that runs diagonally across England. The mightiest peak of the Chilterns, in the neighbourhood of Wendover, does not reach a thousand feet. A
more southerly piece of the chalk, in Hampshire, was described by Gilbert White, as a magnificent mountain, in
a passage that has aroused no little ridicule. Yet Gilbert
White was a scholar and a writer of good sound English as
well as a pioneer in the natural history of birds. The Chilterns are magnificent to those who know them; and the
country in their neighbourhood depends on them, seems to
lean against them as though they were a vertebral chain of
real mountains. Their occasioned barrenness, which is one
of their beauties, is not native and is unexpected. England,
as no student of landscape must forget, began as a forest. At
a time when men of peace were clearing the woods at Berkhamsted and the plains to make farms, the great beech
woods in the Chilterns were the most highly valued of retreats for bandits and freebooters and some of the last of the
woods were destroyed, in the time of James I, in order
to allow the king's writ to run among the surrounding
neighbours. You still feel the support of the Chilterns
though they do not belong to that county in a Hertfordshire lane where the flints in the subsoil may be refined
down to the breadth of a bread knife.

It is easy to exaggerate the influence of strata on scenery of
any low undulating country. Mixed farms are found on

soils, heavy and light, elm and oak and ash and lime and sycamore flourish above chalk or above any igneous rock whatever. The bones that geologists deal with are concealed even within the confines of a parish by coverings that bene﹏ fit particular crops. Human habitations are found wherever water is found. Almost everywhere on the eastern side of England, indeed up to the western fringe, the landscape is so intensely human that you may quite forget the 'rocks', if the geologists' word may be used, of the less stony subsoils. The upper parts of the chalk ridges, the 'magnificent moun﹏ tains', are an exception. The trees and hedges disappear, the clothing is soft sweet grass—marvellously close and springy wherever it has been much trodden and grazed by sheep. When walking the ridge you exult in the wide general view of plain and hill; when below it your eye delights chiefly in the mere shape of the contour as created by aeons of deposit and later denudation.

If you study a guide﹏book to the Chilterns you are likely to find little mention of the range, and a great deal about the river valleys, for in them the villages cluster. The Chilterns are a potent watershed though most of the streams are short. Springs bursting out near the top of the water level have scooped out the land in roughly parallel valleys, all of them fair to see and well populated. The Lea, where still survives an old mill or two, as at the gracious village of Wheat﹏ hampstead; the Mimram, running below a great hill of sand at Codicote, the Gade and Chess which have named the villages of Gaddesden and Chesham are all proper places of pilgrimage in the days of autumn coloration. The Ver is the river of St. Albans or Verulamium and is still beautiful even when among the houses of that historic city. How pleasant are their upper reaches, often broad/ ened into lakes in the parks of the great houses, as at Luton Hoo, Tewin Water and Brocket. How little re/ garded are they when they approach the lower reaches of the Thames in and about London! A stream perhaps only known to Londoners, though unseen, is that which flows inside an iron case above the rails in Sloane Square station.

A good part of the Chilterns is as richly wooded as the Dunstable downs are bare and gives snug harbourage in its dips as well as in its long narrow valleys to large and still beautiful villages, though many pernicious examples of 'ribbon development' deface Buckinghamshire and Oxford hamlets. You meet many examples in crossing the richly endowed spur that separates Beaconsfield from Berkham/ sted. It happens often enough to be accepted as a modern mark of our scenery that a new and not lovely village has been run up alongside the railway, while a pleasant old village is found at a short remove. Thanks to the ease of modern motor transport, the road connecting the unlovely new and the restful old village becomes avenued by bun/ galows, by flimsy and ill/designed houses that are even worse than the village of villas and shops grouped round the rail/ way station and drives an ugly wedge into the old historic hamlet. The neighbourhood of the village of Gray's *Elegy* is no exception. Some are happily saved, as at Harpenden in Hertfordshire, by the penetration of an old common or enlarged green. Buckinghamshire is rich in such greens. One that is spacious and 'advantaged' by trees helps to re/

tain the grace of Redbourn on one side of its busy road, while the other side becomes utterly defaced.

By this village where the ridge is scarcely apparent the elm becomes the prevailing tree; but on most of the higher points of the wooded Chilterns the beech holds its supremacy. At all seasons of the year it enriches the view as no other tree. What green is so freshly green as the 'uncrumpled vernation' of its opening buds? What russet is so rich as those leaves when the green fluid retreats and so discloses the ruddy yellow dyes? Even when they fall (and often they hang on into winter) they gleam like copper on the floor of the woods. When winter comes are any pillars more stately, more brightly frescoed?—and the graceful twigs of the canopy reach out into a delicate pattern much more individual than the dome of full summer foliage. The headquarters of the beech are found not at Burnham, whose avenues have a singularly wide circulation, but at High Wycombe, which remains the centre of a very old local industry, chair making. The woods remain, nevertheless, and the village of West Wycombe, nearby, has become one of the proudest possessions of the National Trust.

The Chilterns which fade away in quiet gradation on the north-east are suddenly cut off on the west. The impatient Thames, hurrying downwards from the west, made short work of the chalk barriers. It cut a gap (as famous as any in the English landscape) between Oxford and Reading. The scenery on the south of the Thames at this point might very well have been like the scenery on the north; but England seldom repeats itself. Berkshire has little in common with Buckinghamshire, and the Berkshire downs and Wiltshire

downs do not suggest the Chilterns. Berkshire is certainly
one of the loveliest and most richly varied of English counties. It has down and wooded hill, plain and river scenery,
great houses and fair villages, and the best of all the green
roads of England. It has much more wood than is common
in England. One of the barer bits of the downs, beautifully
named the Fair Mile, drops on one side towards the
village of Aston Tirrold, into a dip known and well described as Juniper Hollow. On the other side are plentiful
woods of both conifer and beech. Social workers have
noticed how strongly the high down divides the shire. One
side the people look to Oxford as their centre for hospitals
and what not; on the other they acknowledge the claims of
Reading, their own county capital. The Fair Mile is probably an extension, not an integral part of the historic Ridgeway. It has proved irresistible to those whose interest it is to
train and gallop the thoroughbred horse. The green surface
is unmetalled and unhedged, giving fair prospects to every
point of the compass.

If not so sweetly named as those Oxfordshire tributaries
of the Thames, the Evenlode and the Windrush, the Kennet is lovely even when compared with the livelier rivers of
western England. The loveliest reach, if we include the
neighbouring slopes, lies near Newbury. On the one side
the quick declivity is crowned by a relic of old Windsor
Forest. The oaks are as old and immense as those of Hatfield Park and help to envelop, at Aldermaston, one of the
most beautiful of our villages. Commons top the slopes on
both sides, at Crookham (where is the oldest golf links in
England, Blackheath excepted) and on the other Buckle-

bury Common, famous for its avenue of oaks. The road between them leads to Bradfield and the valley of the Pang, a short stream for its size, but as richly meadowed as the Kennet and as well stored with trout.

England does not often repeat itself; but there are family likenesses. A true perception of one of them induced a scenic artist of to-day to imitate his predecessor of two thousand years ago. The Bedfordshire Lion and the Berkshire White Horse decorate very similar ridges; and the Berkshire and Wiltshire downs are cousinly to the Chilterns. The Berkshire horse, though most queerly patterned, is said to indicate points of the horse of its era. Early Celtic art was often not so much imitative as conventional. It liked pattern first and similitude after. There is a glorious pattern of a horse on a gold coin, probably of the fifth century A.D., found at Silchester, which suggests that the Uffington White Horse was its inspiration. This gigantic creature is not an outline, as casual observers have sometimes thought, but a narrow elongation of a patterned horse. The only part that is outlined is the queer bulging jaw. Some say it is not a horse but a dragon; and its stable is close beside, Dragon's Hill, associated later with St. George, who perhaps supplanted a heathen deity. The dragon or horse, or whatever it may be, is certainly of Celtic or Germano-Celtic origin and preceded the Roman invasion. It is unique, though there are fifteen other white horses on the Wiltshire and Hampshire downs. They all date from the eighteenth century when such art became a fashion.

The archaeologists have made very prolonged and careful investigation of the subject and have come to the conclusion

that the White Horse of Uffington in Berkshire, the Long
Man of Woolmington in Sussex and the Cerne Giant at
Cerne Abbas in Dorset are the only hill figures that are of
ancient date. Old, but of course not of a prehistoric date,
are the two crosses cut in the chalk over against Princes
Risborough.

The Uffington White Horse is more famous but perhaps
less scenic than the immense earthen camp over against it.
This was doubtless one of the citadels (peculiar to south and
east England though repeated at later dates in many places)
raised by the immigrant tribes from Germany who began to
arrive in numbers from the fifth century B.C. They were
chiefly used, as is probable, for the protection of flocks, or
on the threat of a raid. How far these were used, adapted
and remade by the Romans who shall decide? But many a
so-called Roman camp is of much earlier origin.

Round about these chalk effigies of lion and horse, the
grass is scored in white streaks which are sometimes roads,
sometimes the relic marks of glissades, where the steep slope
and slippery grass has tempted youth to the game of tobog-
ganing. You can detect the plausibility of the horse and the
skill of the artist only from a distance; and you cannot discover the glory of the downs without regarding them from
below as well as from their peaks. The Vale of White
Horse has inspired a good many writers; but the locus classicus is at the beginning of *Tom Brown's Schooldays*, as the
locus for a description of a Wessex heath is in Thomas
Hardy's *The Return of the Native*.

The Vale might well inspire a writer. It lies between some
low hills or hillocks that help further to separate the chalk

from the limestone, the downs from the wold. No one can
pretend to know England, till he has travelled from Wan-
tage in the direction of Swindon or of Marlboro'. Just before you catch a glimpse of the White Horse's head the road
becomes a beech colonnade so completely pillared and
roofed that it is dark long before sunset. It prepares the way
to a beech wood which is one of the delights of the view
from the back of the Horse. The road along the Vale of
White Horse is as necessary a route for the motorist as the
Ridgeway for the walker. This prehistoric road is the greatest perhaps of all the green roads of England. It gives a
marvellous example of the permanence of certain of the
engineering works of man. It would be a superlative to ask
for a monument of turf in place of Horace's monument of
brass. Even the shallow baulks between the open fields of the
early English cultivators resist the overthrow of devouring
time for century after century. Old British pre-Roman
camps remain ineffaceable in spite of the worm which is
their most efficient enemy. This road, little trodden and entirely unused as a thoroughfare, is hardly less conspicuously
a part of the landscape than the Barnet by-pass or any of
these immense shining roads, with their embankments and
cuttings, that have been driven across England for the sake
of machines driven by the internal combustion engine. The
ridge alongside is in places sharp and regular, but what we
notice is the straight and spacious road itself, distinct in
spite of its complete covering by down grass and its disregard by modern transport. The first engineers took the high
road, the later the low, for there in each era the population
was gathered. The Icknield way, south-west of Hitchin,

went by some of the highest parts of the Chilterns. The Ridgeway is directed by the crown of the Berkshire downs. Up there you are 'wrapt from the world', and must come down to the dips and hollows, though these are often shallow enough, to find the villages. They are less famous than the villages of the Cotswolds; but are lovely nevertheless; and full of character. They are often distinguished from one another by the points of the compass: West Ilsley and East Ilsley and West Hendred and East Hendred are all close together and all characteristic. Unlike Swindon, which has one of the loveliest sites in southern England, they all fit the landscape and seem to belong to it. The site of Swindon, perfect though it is, was chosen for wholly utilitarian reasons. It was a half-way house between London and Bath and suitable in the early railway days for the changing of engines. While in the neighbourhood of the Ridgeway the native grass gives place to tilth, the note of spaciousness is still held. The vast fields are seldom 'ribbed and paled in' by either wall or hedge; and those who seek cover, chiefly sportsmen waiting for driven game, must erect a basket hurdle. Lines of these in some places affect the eye like shacks or allotment huts. Every view is made up of colour as well as of shape; but the colour changes often and quickly during the course of the day as well as of the seasons. Parts of this down country are tinted with a surprising lilac hue; and patches are often thought to be a chalky tilth when in fact they are covered with one of the characteristic down grasses. The seed heads remain throughout the late autumn, the winter and the first months of spring. Drifts of this lilac among the brown and green and white have that sort of

floating atmospheric effect which belongs to shades of blue
and is most often noticed over bluebells in an open wood.
A mixture of colours like none other surprises you as you look
over one slope of the downs near the White Horse where
the lilac grass prevails. It makes a foreground to the further
view of the beechwood in the valley or to the long blue distance towards Oxford. From such a place distance lends
enchantment even to the smoke and steam of a train winding its way along the valley.

Melancholy does not belong to English views, except
where nature has been smirched by art, or degeneration of
the surface is conspicuous. These downs are seldom gloomy
(in spite of Thomas Hardy). They are unspoilt by the
builders, in contrast with some parts of the North and South
Downs, and the few hamlets and homesteads visible from
the crest are generally beautiful. An exception, at least to
some eyes, is the bluff of the downs above Marlboro' and
some of the farms along the Wiltshire and Berkshire border-
line. Oliver Goldsmith wrote with melancholy of the
Deserted Village; but his imagination did not rise to the
vanished village. 'Sweet Auburn' did not know the fate of
Snape. Thereabouts a village clean vanished in sympathy
with the desertion of the land by grain farmers. Grass and
thistles succeeded broad views of grain. A mounted herds-
man succeeded a group of labourers and farmers. Church,
farmhouse, cottage toppled and mouldered away like the
emptied houses of Galway or Constantinople, with an old
railway truck and a shack or two as their only successors.
The barns of neighbouring homesteads went the same
way and townsmen in place of cultivators inhabit the

desolated farmhouses. The note of sadness is expressed in the general view. Neglect is palpable; and this is felt with multiplied force in a country where most of the landscape has been enriched, one may say created, by human care and affection.

Nevertheless the melancholy is being dissipated. Across the lovely valley of the Kennet and above Hungerford, a pleasant valley township, a farming genius (Mr. Hosier) has discovered how to make the down flourish like the rose. Instead of homesteads you see quaint but never ugly open-air bails or steadings. Cattle, which are an addition to any landscape, multiply and even corn begins to lend the green beauty of spring and summer, the gold glory of harvest. Hereabouts the motor-car, which has proved the severest threat in history to the loveliness of England, courses over the short grass and chalk roads in the service of farm operations. The shire horse is more pictorial; but the new down farming has a large balance in its favour, aesthetically as well as in economies. As a rule in down country the trees begin where the level falls. They belong to dips, declivities and valleys. The exceptions are the clumps of beeches and sometimes the firs that the afforesters have planted. The fir woods are not attractive and have an alien look, but the clumps of beeches marvellously fill the eye, and to the voyager bring out the sense of his passage like the stops in a sentence. One could not wish such artificial punctuation away; and often the clump is a relic, not an addition.

Quite supreme among upland woods is Savernake Forest. The chalk downs are not only chalk; and by Savernake a cap of clay gives good hold to the roots of oak as well as beech. Both grow to great size; and the absence of undergrowth from a good part of the great wood adds to the glory of the trunks, for those who drive along the roads, and to the pedestrian who would penetrate into the depths it offers little barrier to movement or even to sight. No chalk-land wood may compare with it.

Not so far off was the first capital of England, probably because the down thereabouts was easily cleared. Avebury is not less impressive than Stonehenge and is probably older. Civilisation must have been well advanced when the engineers carried the immense stones for the temple at Stone-henge all the way from the Prescelly hills in South Wales. The best of the Avebury stones have perished within recent years. Local farmers, ignorant and careless of antiquity, practised an ingenious method of breaking the giant stones in pieces by the joint agency of fire and water; and they used the fragments for making roads and for building. It is scarcely credible that a nation proud of its past could permit such a monument of antiquity to be so desecrated and de-stroyed. Happily, earth was stronger than stone, and less de-sirable. The great mound is said to be the biggest earthwork in the world. It is comparable almost with the Pyramids. Kipling says that Pevensey is fathoms deep in history. Sure-ly no village in England and few anywhere else in the world is so hedged by antiquity as Avebury, built within the arch of the prehistoric earthworks within sight of that artificial mount! And it is a comely village, not unworthy of the aristocracy of its ancestral site. Here is England indeed of to-day and of an unimagined yesterday. The tall stark stones of Stonehenge suggest priestly superstition and priestly con-

Plate 5. An avenue of beeches in Savernake Forest

cern with the stars. Avebury is nearer the earth and the common affairs of men.

The relics of prehistoric civilisation in all this region of the downs suggest that it is holy ground. The circles and vanished stones of Amesbury Hill are only less eloquent than Avebury itself. It was holy ground during the Neolithic culture—round about 2000 B.C.—and long afterwards. It was to the holy house at Amesbury that Queen Guinevere fled and sat weeping with the novice while

> *One low light betwixt them burned*
> *Blurred by the creeping mist; while all abroad*
> *The white mist like a face cloth to the face*
> *Clung to the dead earth and the land was still.*

A short journey from Amesbury brings you into sight of Stonehenge. Avebury at a distance is the more impressive. The great mound dominates the scene. At Stonehenge, mighty though the Sarsens are, they are dominated by the down. But when you come near their majesty is overwhelming. You wonder not only at the physical marvel of the carriage of these fantastic blocks from far Wales and of the placing of the traverses on the uprights. You wonder at the prompting of such a temple. It must have been spiritual. It was raised by a people who had traffic with the heavens as well as with the earth. We know, of course—and not only from the evidence of the two outer stones—that it was oriented (though the word is contradictory) to the setting sun at Midsummer; and we feel that this was more than a mere astronomical essay. It is impossible to look out from those vast pillars at the wide spaces of both earth and sky

c

without a sense of ancient worship. This is holy ground; and something more than a historic or aesthetic sense has at last persuaded our preservers of rural England to remove the unseemly erections near it. They were sacrilegious. Dr. Cornish wishes even the neighbouring trees to be felled because they interfere with the width of the circle of the landscape. Stonehenge is the centre of a universe whose circumference is nowhere. The Sarsens aspire as surely as the towering point of Salisbury Cathedral. Incidentally it is strange that an airman may fly over that spire and not notice it while the Stonehenge circle is like a blazoned signal.

Plate 6. The Salisbury Plain, near Stonehenge

CHAPTER III

The Fens

England slopes much more gently into the shallow North Sea than into the English Channel, though that, too, is of little depth at its eastern end. You know the sea becomes little more than a lagoon or vlei on either side where Holland and England are indented by the twin waters of the Zuider Zee and the Wash. You may know that the sea is shallow by the number of migratory birds that cross it in both directions in both winter and spring for this mysterious movement takes place only over shallow seas and not over deep, as though the birds remembered that once upon a time the gentle valley was a land valley, not a great gulf, a place across which they could slowly drift as the winter stiffened from the north.

The valley of the North Sea, so to call it, rises gently both on the south-western and the north-eastern side; and the Wash has a local likeness to the Zuider Zee. The art and science of reclaiming land from both salt and fresh water were practised earlier on the north sides, and Dutch engineers with some Dutch workmen gave us much of the gloriously fertile plain where Hereward the Wake, 'the last of the English', hid safely in the marshes. Vermuyden, who came over from Holland in the late seventeenth century and was knighted by Charles I, is among the makers of England in a strictly physical sense. Later, in our days the

Dutch brought over the secrets of the cultivation of their recovered soil. They built the first factory for dealing with that marvellous root, the sugar-beet. It makes a singularly salient appearance at Cantley in the lowlands near the beautiful old town of Norwich. It may be described as a part of the scenery. It altered the face of the country at the opening of the twentieth century. It was followed twenty years later by the gleam of glass houses glinting strangely in the sun from unexpected places. The new industry of bulb growing, for which Holland had been famous these hundreds of years, was successfully planted; and new scenes appeared. The black soil became as bright as an Eastern carpet with daffodil and tulip.

Inland of the eastern plain rise clay hills that would not be called hills in other parts of the country; but it happens not once or twice in Britain that the widest views are seen from the lowest ridges. The Great North Road between Huntingdon and Peterboro' runs on one such ridge and gives now and then, for example, near Alconbury Hill, a view so spacious that it seems all distant. Beyond the line of the nearest field and hedgerow stretches the fenland, almost featureless, save for its colour; and these lands have a peculiar gift of colour at all hours, but most at sunrise and sunset.

In all the annals of the English countryside none gives a more persuasive picture of the contrast between the old England, before man had tamed it, than the twelfth-century records of the Crowland monks.

'The whole country was almost dead flat, with here and there an inconsiderable eminence standing up from it. These heights were often surrounded by water, and when the

Plate 7. A bulb farm at Spalding, Lincolnshire

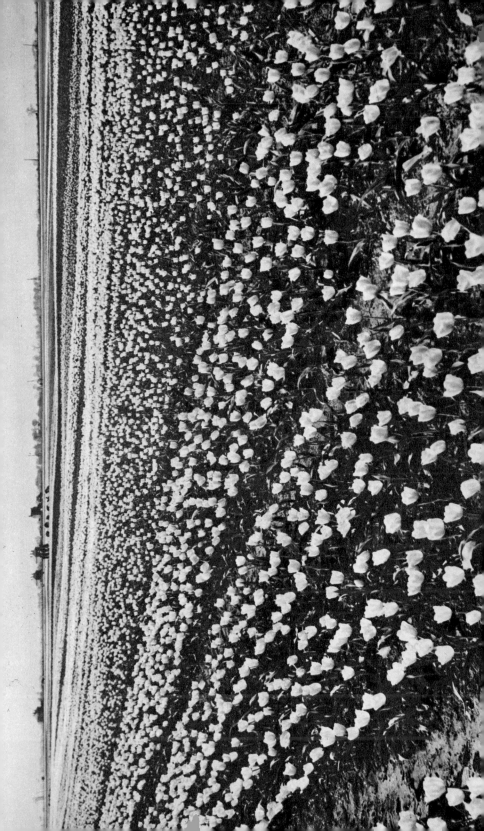

autumnal and spring rains swelled the meres and streams and covered the flats, they formed so many detached islets.

'When were there in the world such eels and eel-pouts as were taken in the Ouse and Cam, close under the walls of the abbey at Ely? (3000 eels, by ancient compact, do the monks of Romney pay every Lent to the monks at Peter-borough, for leave to quarry stone in a quarry appertaining to Peterborough Abbey; but the house of Ely might have paid ten times 3000 eels, and not have missed them, so plenty were they, and eke so good.)

'The streams, too, abounded with pike, and the meres and stagnant waters swarmed with tench and carp.

'Nor is there less plenty of waterfowl and for a single half-penny men can have enough for a full meal.

'Nor was there a lack of fish that came up the river to spawn.

'Of wild boars of the forest in the Fen the head only was served up.

'The wild buck was less abundant in the fenny country.

'It was also facile to snare the crane, the heron, the wild-duck, teal, and the eccentric and most savoury snipe; the swallow-kite, the swarth raven, the hoary vulture, the swift eagle, the greedy goshawk, and that grey beast, the wolf of the Weald.'

In order to keep body and soul together they fell into the custom of the country and became mighty hunters before the Lord. It was a wild and wonderful country of great extent for that little island. The circle of it included a good part of the shires of Huntingdon, Cambridge, Norfolk and Lincoln. It was to become the very richest land within

England. Where the Crowland monks saw the wind
ruffle the waters of sedge and reed you may watch to-day a
puff of breeze ripple a great plain of golden grain that
shifts the light as the ripples of the sea itself. Labourers
with plots scarcely bigger than gardens have founded for-
tunes on the growth of garden produce. Many new crops
have first appeared and flourished there from bulbs of
more than Dutch excellence to sugar-beet and strawberries.
Happily the reformation, the reclamation was not quite
complete. If there is a virgin plot in England, where
neither forester nor farmer has effaced 'the fabric work of
time', it is Wicken Fen in Cambridgeshire; and it is to
be preserved 'in perpetuity' as a sanctuary for bird and butterfly. It is, of course, in some measure pruned and polished
or the sedge and scrub would be too thick and forbidding
even for the wildest of wild birds. There are 'rides' where
the favoured 'mothers' are allowed to sugar cork posts for
the better catching of rarities. A certain thinning both of
sedge and scrub is allowed. The broad dykes of the Dutch
reclaimers are at its edge and add much to the charms
of the scene. The water-lilies are like a cloth of gold, and
from under them in due season emerge great number of
dragonfly, especially the light blue species; and they are
as lovely as the flowers. Some wild plants that had all but
vanished have been replanted: the great water-dock, for
example, which is the host plant of the great copper butterfly that had quite vanished. This too, though not quite
identical with the old English species, has been reintro-
duced.

In several parts of the Fens, stretches of easily flooded lowlands remain, as at Lingay; and without strain to the imagination you may stand thereabouts when the frost is heavy on the land, and recover the sense of the ancient wildness. The best hour is sunset, for the moist air catches up and distributes, almost prismatically, the rays of the setting sun, interrupted only by the boughs of a few stunted willows. The Fens are famous for their sunsets, which to the fenman have become a very part of the landscape. They are as well worth a pilgrimage as Crowland Abbey itself. The chief workers of the miracle were a Dutchman and a Duke, Cornelius Vermuyden and the Duke of Bedford. Great lakes, such as Whittlesea Mere, as well as swamps and marshes, vanished before the combination of engineering skill and a long purse. If the Dukes never recovered the millions they spent they had the satisfaction of creating the most fertile of lands and leaving to their descendants many hundreds of prosperous farms. The Thorney estate is a good example. The abbey and the village, which have seen all these changes, are teed up on a scarcely perceptible but at one time invaluable hill. The place even in this generation was so far feudal, though the Dukes had no residence there, that the cottage tenants, many on a weekly tenure, left their lease by will to their children. The fertile land was one of the first areas sought by the nation for smallholdings, and might have become such a headquarters as now is found by Sutton Bridge and Holbeach, if the plans had gone through.

It would be difficult to find any moderately wide space in England where the landscape has not been vitally changed within the last three or four hundred years; and less pleasant changes are proceeding very rapidly at this moment; but

nowhere else perhaps was the taming of the scene so complete, not only to the eye but in deeper essentials, as over the
Bedford levels, so-called. The water, often called the eye of
scenery, that used to lie in broad meres, was made to flood
into dykes cut so deep that if you skate along them you may
often see nothing but sky and bank. Neither the fish nor the
birds wholly vanished. The dykes are full of coarse fish and
are freely fished by any who please. Snipe still frequent the
fens, but chiefly in the early autumn, and you flush them
not from soggy marshes but from broad acres planted with
potatoes.

When there is a heavy frost the place becomes a Holland
indeed. The dykes are converted into waterways, real means
of communication. The fenmen swinging along in close
lines one behind the other, keeping time with their long
strokes may be likened to migratory duck or geese which
keep a regular formation and reduce the air resistance.
When once you have the freedom of the dykes you may
skate an indefinite distance and some of the dykes that give
access to the great network run up to the railway. They are
more accessible than is generally known. You may, for example, start on a small dyke almost alongside the eastern
platform of Holme station on the main line south of Peterboro' and cover say forty miles of waterway before you come
by way of Chatteris to the Old Nene. If you ask your
way you will be given no place-names but be advised to go
by way of the sixteen-foot and right-handed down the
twenty-four-foot or whatever the breadth of the dyke as
designed by the first engineers.

When you climb the banks you will see a flatland,

broken chiefly by the windmills, first used for pumping the water, and the straight lines of the 'droves' or elevated road-ways. You may find here and there a tree growing on aerial roots. It has survived the sinking of the land level as trees survive the sucking away of the salt in the neighbour-hood of the salt works in Cheshire.

Islands of course there are; the district is a sort of land archipelago. Groves and villages are firmly based where the land rises though ever so little. The bigger waterways are banked up into salient ridges, which replace the ranges of other lands; but you never lose the sense of utter flatness, that prohibits even the river from flowing with any percep-tible force.

A sharp distinction is drawn in popular speech between the flatlands of south Lincolnshire and thereabouts and the more southerly areas. You must not call the Lincolnshire farms fens, nor the Huntingdonshire, marshes. Both words have lost their proper meaning. They speak of the past and record it, like many country place-names. 'England, thou art a fen of stagnant waters,' was written before the great change was consummated. Perhaps the most progressive farming in England and the most prosperous is found on the marshes round about the eastern and northern surround-ings of the Wash. Some small portion of the Wash near Sutton Bridge has been reclaimed, and larger areas just awash at high tide are now ready for reclamation. Per-haps soon they will be added to England. Proposals have been made for vast reclamation schemes, such as those being carried out (on a forty years' scheme) on the Zuider Zee on the eastern side of this shallow sea valley.

Land and sea are merged. A man on a horse can ride out from the north-western shore for some eight miles and not risk wetting his feet. There are banks of silt off King's Lynn that scarcely allow the Ouse to make its way to the sea. The harbour was once the greatest of shipping ports in England for grain, but the glory has departed partly from the shallowness of the water but chiefly because the trade in grain has shifted to Liverpool by the compulsion of eco-nomic events. The granary of England, so far as native acres are concerned, is still in the eastern counties; but a bigger granary, more cheaply farmed, lies across the At-lantic in the prairie provinces of Canada.

No place perhaps is more eloquent of this strange country than Sutton Bridge. A prosperous village lies along the flat straight road. It ends at the river Welland, which lies deep between its piled banks. Timber ships still unload their cargoes there, at the mouth of a formation that might puzzle geologists. A spacious harbour was dug there and entrance gates built, but the treacherous soil refused the burden and the whole structure collapsed. The hollowed harbour is now a very green golf links and you hardly notice where the entrance was designed. Just above this village and the next to the west are very fertile fields on which begin to appear glass-house after glass-house built for the new industry of bulb growing. The smallholders are housed for the most part in comely buildings, many of them roofed with Nor-folk thatch. From the steel bridge that carries the railway over the chasm of the river you may just see where the sea seeps into prospective fields very ready for reclamation.

If you travel from there to King's Lynn you will pass

many acres of plum and other fruit. Both fen and marsh
suit the cultivation of flowers and vegetables; many districts, where the land is a trifle higher are entirely suitable
for fruit. Wisbech, a characteristic and after its manner, a
beautiful riverside town, is one of the headquarters of fruit
growing.

It was in the river at Wisbech that excavators found some
of the most convincing proofs of the queer changes of the
scenery of this part of England. Buried under yards of silt
were the hulls of antique boats; and near by in the clay
underneath were embedded the roots of good-sized trees.
Beyond question the level of the land has changed not once
but at various dates; and the evidence of old forests is overwhelming. The Fens silted up before they were drained. The
same sort of change occurred, as is probable, in the black
land, very suggestive of the eastern Fens, that is found to the
north of Liverpool, especially by Blundellsands. Where
now great yields of corn are gathered, where potatoes and
cabbage give good rewards, foresters as late as the time of
King John were the chief farmers. Lancashire and Cambridgeshire have this degree of unexpected likeness.

The Fens proper as we know them, are not three hundred
years old. Changes began with the building of the great
abbeys and the monasteries: such as Ramsey, Crowland
and Thorney, in a land that had remained until the twelfth
century much as the ancient Britons knew it. Ely—a word
that means willow tree—was a real island standing up in the
midst of lakes and meres that allowed no apparent passage
on foot. In the monastic records is much quaint evidence of
the nature of the country. The abbeys made most of their

payments in kind: eels and stone were an easier and better
medium than gold and silver. The monasteries added a good
deal by reclamation to the lands they possessed; and one of
the earliest dykes took its name from a mediaeval bishop.
The Romans, whose engineering zeal was insatiable, appear to have heaped up soil over some sunk acres near the
west side of the Wash and the high droves, running to-day
across the Fens, are successors to Roman Causeways. Yet the
old descriptive terms of fear, such as other natives have be-
stowed on forests, were still justified. A 'great and hideous
Fen' covered all this district as forbiddingly as the hated
forest in other parts. Cornelius Vermuyden with the Duke
of Bedford altered all this as we have seen. At the beginning he was bitterly opposed by Oliver Cromwell, who
lived for a while at Hinchinbroke, one of the loveliest
country houses in England and lovelier than ever after the
ingenious reparations and additions made by Lord Sand-
wich at the end of the nineteenth century. Happily the
Protector reversed his own action as a young agitator,
and the scheme of Vermuyden and the Dutchmen went
through. It was progressive. Four successive Dukes of
Bedford spent money and energy on the reclamation. When
it was over the whole great area of nearly 700,000 acres,
most of it known as the Bedford Level, was cut up by
dykes and dotted with windmills. Courses of the very
rivers, especially Ouse and Nene and Cam were multiplied and altered. The landscape was remade.

In some mining districts language has become so far
changed that a mound of soil is called a fosse. What has
been dug out, being conspicuous as a hill, has taken the

name proper to the hole or ditch. So in the Fen landscape
the dyke is seen as a ridge. The great mound at Avebury is
said to be the biggest earthwork in the world; but it is a
little thing compared with the great hundred-foot drain as
seen between Erith and Downham Market. The banks rise
in places to the height of a church; and they run in a per-
fectly straight line for nearly thirty miles. The dyke dominates the landscape over a good part of this great distance.
Some ingenious men of science fathered here an experiment
for demonstrating that the earth was round; and the passage
of a ship along this drain, so to call it, was long enough—
and with room to spare—to serve their demonstration. The
scale is almost of fantastic grandeur; and perhaps we may
take it as symptomatic of the continuity of English history
that this vast engineering feat was carried out in succession
by the two bitterest rivals in our national history: Charles
I and Oliver Cromwell. The expense was reduced by the
use of prisoners of war; and some partial and feeble attempt
to imitate the Protector's example was made alongside the
Wash in the Great War, when German prisoners were used
for the latest effort at reclamation.

The great and hideous Fen became a Holland for richness, yet Vermuyden made great mistakes from which the
scene has not yet fully recovered. One may say that he was
so fond of land that he forgot the sea. His rivers and dykes
could barely deliver their waters into the sea, until our own
famous engineer Rennie took the lower courses in hand.
The struggle remains. You still may see here and there rising
strangely over the mud banks, bits of queer machinery,
some dredging, some stirring up the mud so that the silt is

Plate 8. Mildenhall Fen, Cambridgeshire

carried seawards. What a kaleidoscope it would be if you could see a film of the centuries: first a great forest that presently fell into the floods. Then lake and marsh of immense extent with low islands rising out of it. On these, towns, villages and houses were built, and those who lived there were fishers and fowlers, not farmers; and how bitterly their successors fought against the Dutch drainers! The monks, for all the wealth of their hunting estates, began to dig ditches and to reclaim. Such schemes have been in existence ever since the Romans landed. The dissolution of the monasteries by Henry VIII stopped all such work and many of the great abbeys that stood up like fortresses began to crumble into ruin. At last in the seventeenth century private persons (known as the Adventurers) began to undertake large plans and the kings took a hand. Between the dykes, cut as straight as the streets of New York, a rich cornland superseded the marsh and lake, and the curious flat beauty of the scene was dotted at every turn by the sails of windmill pumps. The last of these has disappeared in our day, for steam and electricity are more regular than the wind. The corn itself gave way to less pictorial crops, to vegetables and sugar-beet and potatoes. The one constant quality through all the changes, since the forests vanished, is the atmosphere that belongs to flatland and so beautifies all that it enfolds, that a modern art critic has said extravagantly that nothing is so lovely in a picture as mud and reeds.

CHAPTER IV

East Anglia

The Fens intrude into five counties, and are cut off from the North Sea by parts of Norfolk and Suffolk, which have a common name in East Anglia, sharing it with that dwindling portion of Essex which is not smirched by London. Time was when Essex was the granary of London and could completely supply its needs in wheat. The history of all three counties in their relation to national husbandry implies some at any rate of the features of their landscape. They abound in rather flat and heavy fields; and the two qualities are connected. The great ridges of the west, especially in Wales and in Westmorland and Cumberland comb out the rain clouds, stuffed with Atlantic water, and when the west winds reach the east they drive before them harmless wisps of cirrus and stratus cloud. Like sailing ships or woolly sheep the white clouds race overhead, interrupting the sun as little almost as the passage of a great bird. The rainfall is small. Between the driest acres in Essex and the wettest in Cumberland is a difference of a hundred inches of rain in a year. The plain and ordinary fields of Coggeshall, which is near the centre of the driest patch, flame into unbelievable splendour when summer comes, for here and here alone, will certain flower and vegetable seeds surely ripen. The sweet peas, the roses, the kale, the seed wheat are evidence of the hours of sun and

47

Plate 9. A village in the heart of agricultural Essex,
Finchingfield

the absence of rain which are among the distinctions of East Anglia. One of the greatest pictorial botanists of his generation, who lived in the east of England, retired when he had completed the drawing of the whole of the English flora. After long thought and persistent enquiry he decided that the most blessed spot for a man's retirement was the Malvern Hills. He would atone, he thought, in his later years, for the flatness of the land where he had spent his working life. It was not till he was well settled in his new home that he came to see how imperceptive he had been of one of the chief virtues of his native district: it was dry and sunny beyond any region of the west. Because of this soil and scenery and clime most of the pioneers in husbandry have come from the east. Coke of Norfolk and in a less degree that retired politician who was known as 'Turnip Townshend', were subdued, like the dyer's hand, to that they worked in. Theirs was a land that man had to make, not a place where rich grass grew whether you wished it or not, as in Hereford, but a dry plain that flourished or waned according to the work exercised upon it. Some bits of the scenery have been completely changed within this generation. The botanists discovered a curious grass—a hybrid between an American and English variety of the same species—that had a peculiar affinity for land lying low and brackish with sea water. As Marram grass with its incredibly long white roots will penetrate into sand dunes and bind them to a certain constancy, as you may see on many a western links, this spartina grass will consolidate and raise heavy soil that has been half awash and win it for the island. The grass appeared first on the south coast and has flour-

ished greatly at Poole in Dorset, but it has nowhere exercised its craft to more purpose than on some of the marshes
that separate agricultural Essex from the sea. We have
laments from time to time of coast erosion, and they are true
enough of certain districts; but on balance the lands of England grow a little more extensive each year. The cliffs, made
chiefly of so-called slipper clay, keep tumbling into the sea
by Cromer and Runton. The stuff of trenches dug for defensive purposes in 1914 lies to-day either below the sea or in
uncomely heaps on the shore. It is rumoured that the bells
of a church ring below the sea off Aldeburgh, and in our
generation a complete church by Cromer, of which for
many years about half stood forlornly on the cliff's edge, has
wholly vanished. It was a melancholy sight; but the losses
here are more than made good elsewhere; as the story of
other districts will make plain. In Kent, much more emphatically than in Essex, the sea becomes land; and shingle
does in one place what spartina grass, sea holly or marram
help to do in others.

The desert and the sown lie cheek by jowl very sharply
contrasted all about Norfolk. Woods and belts of pine and
furzy commons edge barley fields as closely as hedges in the
Midlands. Yet even sharper contrasts are met by the sea. As
characteristic an example as you could wish is to be seen at
Brancaster. On one side of the little village a high tide completely metamorphoses the scene. The stream and marshland vanish into a lake, and a stranger might fear that the
days of Deucalion and Pyrrha, or of Noah and his wife,
were in danger of returning. The quaint, delightful golf
links appear from some angles to be marooned. On the

D

Plate 10. Ploughing on the Norfolk uplands

other side of the village where the land slopes gradually up
are gracious corn lands and sheep lands and all that farmers desired before the days of cheap grain from overseas.
Some of the well-built homesteads tell the historic tale. As
you travel east from Hunstanton and Brancaster the margin
of the sea becomes fuller and fuller of phenomena scarcely
to be found elsewhere. Parts of it, not least near Wells, are
the paradise of wildfowl, but for the wild fowler. Lurk-
ing in the rushy flats at twilight hours when the flocks of
wild geese and duck flight between feeding and roosting
ground he feels aloof even from the neighbourhood of the
tame and civilised. At this point and that, curiosities of
structure leap to the eye of the least observant. Several Norfolk rivers and streams have habits peculiar to themselves. It
is a trouble to the Ouse and Welland to find a free way into
the Wash, but they take a more or less direct course. These
Norfolk streams when they have made their way almost to
the sea are suddenly halted and must turn abruptly running
almost parallel with the shore which may be no more than
a few yards distant. When they at last break into the sea a
spit of various breadths—and it may be several miles in
length—appears, separated from the mainland by a wide
space at high tide. The spit may be of sand or of shingle.
The most characteristic of the sandy spits is at Blakeney, and
there the spectacle of the incoming or outgoing tide is in
itself worth a pilgrimage. The sea runs up the stream as if it
were itself a stream. The trickle becomes a full river and the
full river, no longer, in Horace's phrase, uxorious, over-
flows the low places in the banks till the flats become a
pattern of full dykes and at last, it may be, a salt lake. The

terns or sea-swallows come inland with the tide, and in a trice the village is a seaside place. Two spots are perhaps more famous than others: Scolt Head, which is a peninsula, in very truth, like Tennyson's Sirmio, an 'almost island' and Blakeney Spit. Scolt Head is one of the very few places in England that has been thoroughly surveyed in all its aspects: its geology, its tides, its changes in history and especially its flora and fauna. Wicken Fen alone can be compared with it in this regard. A place of such rare physical qualities is host to both rare plants and rare birds; and thus both the Spit and the Head being greatly desired by naturalists, have been made into sanctuaries secured in perpetuity. The Cley marshes also give an easy harbourage to rare birds and plants which both show signs of multiplying. The flocks of tern, the great herons standing by their reflections in the shallow waters, the bright stone-crop and tall reeds play the part of trees in an inland landscape. As in the fenland, the churches thereabouts stand out in regular salience; they have been immortalised in the architectural pictures.

The abrupt round hills between Runton and Sheringham are not more definitely a part of the landscape than Beeston Church. Men see scenery through the glass of their own particular interest. To sportsmen Norfolk is either a wild marshland haunted by wildfowl or a highly tilled countryside divided by belts of fir or fir woods. To a larger holiday-seeking public Norfolk is a county of Broads, a word and scene belonging peculiarly to this part of Britain. They may be called lagoons or meres or even lakes but have their own distinctions. There is one small Broad which is in

essence a lake or a tarn or what you will, for it is uncon-
nected with a waterway. It is a place of singular peace and
retirement where the water-lilies serve as platforms for young
seagulls at their early ventures and the fish scarcely trouble
to move from the passage of your boat or punt. It is the
quietest sanctuary in the island. Most of the rest of the
Broads conceal the presence of streams, mostly sluggish and
moderately deep; and give scope for a sort of yachting that
has few parallels elsewhere. In the area of the Broads (con-
tained within a triangle of which Yarmouth, Norwich and
North Walsham are the points) the wide sails of the wher-
ries appear in quaint distinctness upon the plain, and often
seem to be moving across dry lands. The streams up
which they sail are sometimes separated by narrow chan-
nels or ditches from the reedy Broads. Sometimes the
streams bisect them, as at Hickling Broad, the greatest
sanctuary in the land. Reed and sedge and patches of tussocky grass interrupt the water surface and give shelter and
nesting homes to birds small and great, to bearded tits, to
bittern, to harriers, to duck and wading birds of all sorts,
which are a very part of its being. Here, too, the landscape
varies with the season more abruptly than elsewhere, not
so much because of the flowering of the reeds or such natural
phenomena as from the intervention of harvesting. As you
walk down from the well-treed village of Woodbastwick
with the Broadland alongside, the justness of your expecta-
tion of the scene will depend on the activity of the reed cut-
ters; and the reaping of this harvest alters the scene at least as
completely as the mowing of the corn in the Fens.

No river is more characteristic than the Bure. It is broad

and deep enough for pleasant sailing boats; and the inland village of Horning may be called a yachting centre. It passes through Broad after Broad, including Hickling itself; and others that are smaller and more private have back doors into it. You can scarcely sail along it without coming in sight of what is most characteristic in the natural history of this strange district as well as its scenery. The bittern may boom in your ears and the swallowtail butterfly flutter against your sails. It is perhaps the most typical, as the Little Ouse, especially from its banks is the most pictur-esque.

There is no high ground in the eastern counties. Did not land drainage on any large and official scale begin in Essex and spread from there to the Fens? Here the great Vermuy-den, who retrieved the Fens, made his first and most famous venture. Yet in spite of the slight gradations of contour, the variety of scene can scarcely be exaggerated. The shallow beach by Runton made of 'slipper' clay and flat rock and rough sand and pebble, gives place a few miles to the west, at Weybourne, to a shore where big ships may sail within a stone's throw or less of the land. You may walk in short space from the Salthouse marshes either to a dry waste of iron sand, scarcely giving sustenance to gorse or heath, or to the groves of pleasant trees, of oak as well as pine, that make Holt and its neighbourhood as fair as the beech woods of Buckingham. It is often forgotten that Coke of Norfolk, the greatest of pioneers in our agriculture—both in the breeding of sheep and cultivation of farmland—altered the landscape strangely and permanently by his planting of firs on the seaward side of Holkham.

Plate 11. *The Norfolk Broads*

A much wider, but not a more startling change, has been taking place progressively on the waste and sandy land about the boundary line of Norfolk and Suffolk, where the Forestry Commission has been engaged in one of its largest and most vital ventures. It was once said in relation to parts of Brandon and Thetford that the most conspicuous object in the scenery was the rabbit. On the honeycomb of his warrens the Commission descended. Tens of thousands a month were killed, till extensive areas were cleared and wired off and seedling firs planted behind the ploughs that levelled the warrens. Neat little homesteads were built for the foresters and the afforesters and a rather grim mono-tonous conifer forest was substituted for the old world variety. A new landscape arose, to the admiration of some, to the angry offence of many local persons: the county they had loved was ruined. Protests were loudest about the neighbourhood of Breckland, sometimes said to share with Wicken Fen the honour of being virtually virgin. What Breckland used to be, it remained; and was still peopled by birds and plants that had else disappeared.

What may Breckland mean? The word may be used to describe a sort of landscape as well as to label a particular and peculiar district. Locally or through a long history the sandy fields were known as Brecks, a word of greater anti-quity than the philologists can penetrate; and the district was christened Breckland little more than a generation ago by that fine naturalist, Mr. W. G. Clarke. In prehistoric days, like many other empty parts of England, it was sin-gularly populous and is to-day more thinly populated than any district in the east of England. The geology of this strange area is hardly less obscure than its name; and it is enough perhaps for the student of scenery to know that sand has been crumbled out of the clay and lies in a shallow layer over the surface. It is one of the few places in England where land erosion due to wind is experienced and can be seen in action. The surrounding forests and the curious hedges made of dwarfed Scotch pine (sometimes as broad almost in trunk as in height) have now prevented the wholesale carriage of the surface from one farm to the next; but the small sandstorm is not unknown.

This strange district by Thetford and Mildenhall is, like Pevensey, 'fathoms deep in history.' Its bare heaths and sandy farms and wide patches that belong neither to the desert nor the sown to-day harbour very rare plants, many held to belong exclusively to the seaside. They have diminished and might have been wholly extinguished like the rare birds and insects, if economic afforesters had enjoyed free play or carried through their full programme. Happily, Norfolk naturalists intervened in time, and by Lakenheath a characteristic piece of Breckland has been saved for posterity. The populous haunt of neolithic man continues to nourish its strange grasses and clovers, and remain a haunt for the ringed and thick-kneed plovers.

A part of Breckland belongs to Suffolk; but as you travel southward towards London the country of pine and heath gives place to agricultural land such as you may find in any county of England. Some parts of it have yielded the secret of their quality to both poet and painter. No one has drawn a more telling picture of his native place, the marshy wastes behind Aldeburgh, than Crabbe; and few, if any bits of England have, so to say, a wider circulation than the neighbourhood of Stratford St. Mary and Dedham, where Constable used to be sent out by his master, the miller, to study the ways of the wind as told by the clouds.

The mills on Stour or Waveney or other quiet streams belong to the landscape as do the tall spires, the sailing clouds, and, may one say, such rainbows as crowned the harvesters in Constable's famous picture. Rivers are the county boundaries. Suffolk is a Mesopotamia, but they make no sort of division in the scenery. The whole of East Anglia is knit by a common likeness. Norfolk and Suffolk, both, compete with Wiltshire for the leadership of English agriculture. There grow the best barleys and there were bred the redpoll cattle and the Suffolk down sheep and the Suffolk 'Punch' heavy horse. The charm of the most ancient of industries is for the most part unsullied by industrialism. Are there any counties where country houses of such antique peacefulness are found? The doubly moated home of Helmingham where still the drawbridge is raised nightly may stand as example. The wealth of the district came from agriculture—in much more bounteous measure —in days when sheep carried golden fleeces. We come across evidence of the fine liberality of the wealthy wool merchants in Oxford and many another county; but no more graciously English examples could be found than the church and other buildings at Lavenham and Long Melford. Both villages supply monuments of national history surviving from days when architecture was an art indeed.

The east of England is not a region of great trees, and indeed almost everywhere the sea is an enemy to trees; but the trees multiply and increase in stature towards the south, and into London itself is thrust as pleasing a forest as the county contains. The verderers and agisters and the rest who control Epping Forest have preserved for the wood and open spaces much of its early glory. It is wild though sub⁄urban; and the multitude of hornbeams that peculiarly flourish there are twisted into as strange gargoyle shapes as say the antique olive trees of Majorca. A fresh air blows and the woodland scents are perceptible even on the busy net⁄work of main roads. It is some test of the purity of its air that a strange plant, half seaweed, half moss flourishes there but is wholly absent from big towns. There is no single lichen within the inner circle of London. In Epping, like the rocks at the seaside, the trees are freely coloured with its grey⁄green dyes.

CHAPTER V

The Wolds

An immense distance separates the Cotswolds from the downs, though they run parallel and side by side; and from the wold you may see the White Horse across a slender valley. The wold and the down are as different as chalk from cheddar. The wolds in one respect are very stark for a bit of England. One of the best books on them, at any rate in expressing their influence on the emotions, is called *Wold Without End*, and if the play on words be forgiven it suggests the first impression of that stern plain on the top of the limestone ridge. Ghosts of a forgotten past haunt both down and wold. The vast mounds at Avebury, which may be called the first capital city of Britain and the stiff skeletons of the stones of Stonehenge have their likeness in the barrow high above Bourton-on-the-Water. Though it is small and unremarkable beside the others, the barrow has a weight of antiquity not exceeded by the more famous monument of the past. On approaching it, the mind is strangely possessed with the sense of:

> *Old unhappy far off things,*
> *And battles long ago.*

and a confession of this mood does not come only from the moody and sentimental. The burial mound copies the spirit of the place. One must not exaggerate the starkness of the uplands, for a great deal of it is good or sufficiently good cornland, and harvest is as rich a spectacle there as in the Fens or the Lothians. What you do not find is the gentle, warm, garden-like appearance that belongs to farm and fields in the counties where hedgerows prevail. The essential quality of the Cotswolds is the strong contrast of a stark landscape with the most humane and lovely villages in the round world. The villages and homesteads, however homely, belong to the ground out of which they have arisen as lichen belongs to rocks. Their nearest likeness, if there is any likeness, is the snow igloos of the Esquimaux. The plain reason is that they were built out of the stone on which they were founded; but the architects who quarried the native stone had the village spirit. They were creating a unit, a community of homes, that belonged to England as to no other country. It is wholly proper and according to the nature of things that one Cotswold village after another is named after the nature of the place where it was built, for each village partakes of the quality of its surroundings and foundations; and largely for this reason is supremely pleasing to the eye and sense. The local people, following the christeners, are particular even about the prepositions and the articles, which they have a tendency to omit. The names are themselves a delight, because they bring up a picture of the site: Stow-on-the-Wold, Moreton-in-Marsh; Bourton-on-the-Water and Bourton-on-the-Hill; Upper Slaughter. There is even Hinton-in-the-hedges at a point where the Cotswold country begins to fade into other England. Not long since it was thought wise by authority to alter some of the county and parish boundaries; and it was found that

local feelings were outraged because under the new arrange/
ment the valley people were associated with the hill people;
and neither approved of such an unnatural association. So
completely, even to-day, in the midst of the frantic efficiency
of transport and annihilation of distance and of frontiers the
people hold to the fidelity of this earthly paradise. You can/
not just visit the Cotswolds and admire the scenery. A
more intimate touch is necessary. One dweller in the Cots/
wolds, newly caught by the charm of the district, wrote to a
friend to say that she now needed a prospect where 'there
was plenty of room for the moon'. The queer excellence of
the phrase will suggest one attribute of the uplands. The
houses belong not only to the rocks beneath them: they are
in touch with their sky, they are at home in space.

The beauty of the names of the villages belongs also to the
rivers that have their source there, Evenlode and Windrush
and the Thames; rivers strangely different from Lea and
Kennet, lustier though not lovelier, trailing clouds of glory
from their source. The ridge whose outlook gave plenty of
room for the moon was at Idbury; the ridge thereabout used
to look over the very spacious forest of Wychwood, once
famous as a home of romance, not to say the haunt of rob/
bers. Now the English landscape and the English farm has
been made by the destruction of forest. The scenery was
created by hard fighting against scrub and wood. The early
forest was a repellant thing, beloved as little by wild birds as
by man, though a favourite with wolves and bandits. We
must rejoice that the early English were iconoclasts; and
even 'the men of the trees' would agree. That struggle came
to a virtual end in the seventeenth century; and too little

Plate 12. A Cotswold stream. The mill at Fairford,
Gloucestershire

rather than too much wood remained. Only the engrooved farmer (who hates even the scattered trees in parkland) would destroy remaining woods; and in this class was Arthur Young, prince of farming critics, though an unsuccessful farmer himself. In fact, owing to his suggestion, a great part of Wychwood was cut and grubbed for the making of agricultural land. A glorious piece of Cotswold scenery vanished and the majority perhaps of those who have tried to farm the cleared spaces regret the Young policy. The fragment of the wood is a treasure.

Lovers of Cotswold dispute its glories. Its most eloquent and most sympathetic critic, Mr. Massingham, author of *Wold Without End*, denies the claim of the counties of Oxford, Warwick and Worcester to hold the true Cotswold mystery. However that may be, and whatever the general superiority of Gloucester, there is one spot which must hold a certain pre-eminence for the more casual pilgrim if not for the initiates. Sudden clefts and wedge-shaped hollows belong to the north-looking edge of the Cotswold Hills and they are in contrast with the long easy comely slope which leads down to the spacious town of Cheltenham. None of the dips is more gloriously sudden than the slope on which Broadway is built. The road is like a stream of water going over a cataract; and might well, like Wordsworth's cataract in the lakes, haunt you like a passion. It is not that the hill is impossibly steep or may compare with hills in North Devon: it is the quickness of the change of view and mood. In a moment, in the twinkling of an eye, the rich monotony of the down breaks into sheer homeliness. The beech trees on the left of the road are like an opening door that lets you

in from the stern world to a warm house. It is perhaps chiefly because of this approach, and of the sudden pleasure that
the grouped houses inspire, that Broadway has earned, in
the mouth of the general public at home and overseas, the
reputation of the loveliest village in the land. Owing to its
fame, it is now over-manicured in some parts; and at the
valley end it is damaged by modern 'concrete mendacities',
but it can never fail to delight the lover of scenery. It is most
beautifully pitched, and apart from the wider aspect it gives
glimpses between the houses that turn the street into a country lane. There are many views of the sort, such as the first
sight of Northleach from the upland, or the upper road into
Burford, coloured with the native stone that went to the
making of many Oxford colleges; but the descent into
Broadway deserves its eminence. One must not dogmatise
on rival merits. Dogberry was right, and comparisons are
odorous. Who shall compare the comfortable domesticity
of Hamerton in Huntingdonshire, or the little gem of
Georgeham in Devon, or Luccombe in Somerset with
Broadway? Lovely villages dot all the English shires; but in
any list of villages the Cotswold country would give the
greatest number of entries. In architecture and fitness of
colour and form Chipping Campden is by itself. One may
look forward to a first glimpse of it from above as one would,
say, to a first sight of the Zambesi Falls or any other wonder of the world. Stow-on-the-Wold boasts an incomparable individuality. It has no parallel. It has filtered their
starkness from the downs without losing the spirit. All the
Bourtons are friendliness incarnate as belongs to houses in
sheltered crevices. You would say that all the villages are

subdued to that they come from, like Bradford-on-Avon, where houses on the cliff above the stream and the antique chapel, look like an outcrop of stone. That, too, is as neces-sary a place of pilgrimage for those who seek out the secret of English scenery as Stratford-on-Avon itself.

One of the great views from the uplands is over the broad park-like valley plain in which Stratford is set. The place has been called the physical centre of England, so far as so eccentric an island can be said to possess a centre; and the view is the right view. There is no woodland, but you can-not find an untreed acre over all that ample prospect. You might be at the edge of the forest of Arden. It recalls that penetrating criticism made by General Botha when he first travelled to London from the south coast. 'I always thought', he said in effect, 'that I was just coming to a forest.' Such is the beneficent legacy of the evil woods that our ancestors cleared.

After absorbing such a view from the top or the slopes of Sunrising Hill, notorious in the annals of motorists, it is a shock to drive into the valley town where every approach, except along the Warwick road on the far side, has been shorn of trees to make room for houses as out of character with the place and with any Shakespearean quality that is left, as the perverted taste of man could devise. This westerly view from the neighbourhood of Edgehill is one of a num-ber of spacious and very English prospects. The next, as you move from escarpment to escarpment in a south-westerly direction, is over the plain first of Evesham and then of Pershore. It is a view that in spring should attract thousands of pilgrims. At the season when plum trees blossom, both valleys are bridal. The white petals lie like snow in hollow after hollow. Nursed by the sun, protected by the hills and favoured by a rich soil, fruit trees grow here or hereabouts as in few English places. In this regard Worcester excels per-haps even Kent or Cambridge. The orchards are loveliest from above, though on a nearer view you receive the sort of treat that is given by a bluebell wood, where the carpet of one colour is covered by a fretted roof of another. Under the fruit trees are sometimes grown not fruit but flowers, wall-flowers for example, and at least two senses are gratified. Evesham, with the relic of its abbey, is a gracious town in itself; but here, as in most English country scenes, it is the prevailing industry that sets the flourish on the scene. The Pershore plum adds as much to these vales in April as the wheat plant to the Fens in August.

Worcester gives place to Gloucester as Warwickshire gives place to Worcester. The hills are not less high and glorious when you come to the great mound from which Stroud is best seen. Within sight below are two rivers of fame, the Avon and the Severn into which it flows. One cannot say of this view that the industries have added the chief enchantment, or for that matter any enchantment; but it is at any rate interesting to perceive how industry that left the Cotswolds, when in Elizabeth's reign sheep ceased to be a source of wealth, found a new home in the watered valleys. Nor are the many factories an eyesore. Some fit harmoniously enough into the view and perched agreeably on the hill:

> Watch the laughing valley hie
> Its business to fulfill.

Yet the wider prospect belongs for once in a way more to nature than to art. The blue hills of Wales, the rounded mounds of the Malverns, the hollowed lines of the river are as God made them, at least in the general pattern.

The wold is the wold; and the Cotswolds mean the high land, a region of stern qualities, that must be learnt to be properly loved. The village of villages belonging to the whole upland range may be proud of its title, Stow-on-the-Wold. Chipping Campden has great architectural rich-ness and unity. Broadway is more cunningly situated. Bur-ford has more variety; the Bourtons are of a homelier nature perhaps; Northleach has incomparable buildings; but if one village is to be taken as type of the Cotswolds, it is Stow-on-the-Wold. It looks as if it rose from the hill in natal completeness, like Athens from the sea. It was pre-conceived when the stone was formed.

Stow-on-the-Wold is wholly Cotswold; but there are two sorts of villages belonging to the region; and it is vain to weigh their comparative merits. There are the wold vil-lages, not very numerous and the valley villages. The hill people will say contemptuously of Bibury itself that it is not Cotswold: it is just a valley village; but the spirit of the Cotswold nevertheless runs down to the skirts of its cloth-ing. It runs down in greatest profusion, like roof water from a church gargoyle, along the course of the Coln. The vil-lages are as proud of their stream as Stow of the wold. Coln St. Aldwyn, Winson, Coln Rogers, Coln St. Dennis are found on either side of Bibury, the precious setting of a jewel. Bibury is a Mecca, for Americans as for Britons; and it could not be otherwise. It has every attribute that

E

Plate 13. Barns on a typical Cotswold farm; Arlington

makes the Gloucestershire village supreme. The Arlington Row, now preserved in perpetuity, exhibits as clearly as if it were a diagram on a school blackboard, how the quarrying of the native stone bred a native school of designers. That line of successive gables sharply angled into the grey roofs but still a part of the grey walls illustrates a style of architecture that deserves a generic name. It is early English, not decorated. It is perpendicular, not Norman; and if domestic architecture deserves such titles as are given to ecclesiastical architecture, it should be suitably christened.

In front of the gables are comely cottage gardens coming up to the road; and across the road is the little river, bridged as a river should be. Yet this is only a branch of the village. You might enter from the other side and say what a lovely village, if you failed to find the Arlington cottages and the bridge over the river. Does any church in any village so belong to its village? Its God's acre is not fenced off from Rectory or school. It is, if you please so to call it, a village garden, a village rose garden; and the roses climb the old stones of the church itself as though to the manner born. Within the church you may scarcely admire its architecture for the views of sunny greenness that are framed by the open doors.

The church has other companions. A very English park comes close to it. And what is an English park? It has a great gate that suggests both peace and privacy. It is a type of the surrounding country of which the chief quality is a little exaggerated as an artist will emphasise the essential: the single trees are more numerous than in the fields. Their broad lowest boughs are raised high enough from the

ground to miss the heads of the cattle and prohibit (as Dar-
win noted) illicit grazing. The Park is a part of a farm of
which the manorial owner has decreed that the beauty is
enough; why trouble about use? A tree is worth much
more than the grass it may destroy. How should it not be
that in the English country house a grace of civilisation has
been reached that is beyond all comparison! If not superior
to any other, it is different from any other largely because its
denizens put enjoyment of the country itself in the forefront
of their affections. How many châteaux in France are one
room thick, are diaphanous and for this reason delightful in
summer! But you know by their structure that they are not
made for a winter home, just as you know in many of these
English country houses, especially the Georgian, that they
are meant to be a solid comfort in the darkness of Decem-
ber. If Gilbert White had lived in Bibury the treed ridge
above it would have been only less famous than the famous
Hanger. The village is sheltered by the Cotswolds, and
aware of the hills from which its stone is quarried.

You must grant the supremacy of Bibury; but all its
neighbours—and the villages are very close together along
the Coln—have a selection of its virtues with individual
works that cannot be rivalled. The building itself, however
humble, matters supremely. The local shops, the local post
offices are themselves cottages, and scarcely distinguishable.
The commercial window or protuberant front was not a
thing envisaged or perpetrated by the Cotswold artist.

You pass into a very different world when you begin to
ascend from the river valley. A favourite exit for pilgrims
to Bibury—and they are many—is by the Fosse Bridge and

the Fosse Way. Below the roads and lanes indicate a pursuit of 'the delicate and gentle art of never getting there'.
Here the upper road goes straight as a homing rook. It is
more suggestive of the Romans than the English; and it
takes you to their famous camp of Cirencester, now, as be-
fits its environment, a centre of agricultural instruction. The
farm thereabouts is more than the wold or the river.

The character of these Cotswold villages is a singularly
true character from whatever angle we regard it. They have
grown out of their native soil like trees. Not one but scores
of villages possessed their own quarry or 'quay', many of
them, as at Burford and Bourton-on-the-Hill, beautiful
places, an addition to the pleasure of the scene. The colour
of the villages is native, is racy of the soil; and often
material for roof as well as wall was dug on the spot. You
do not see the outcrop of stone but what is bred in the bone
will out. Even slate can have the attraction of fitness in its
right place, as you may see in some of the churchyards of
North Wales. In strict aesthetics, unqualified by thought,
the slate headstones are as suitable as marble is unsuitable, is
even hideous.

The presence of this grey stone beneath their feet encouraged the builders to architectural ambitions from a very
early date. Historians tell us that a distinct Cotswold style of
architecture, for house and barn, if not for church, was in
being in the fourteenth century. It continued to develop its
individuality for several centuries, thanks in part to the
wealth of the wool merchants, who built themselves magnificent mansions. They were never alien or fussy. Castle,
mansion, farmhouse, cottage, and barn remained faithful to

the native stone, the native craft and art. The steep roofs, the mullioned windows, the strong walls, are as native almost as the colour of the stone which sets the final flourish on almost every village and farmstead. Cotswold architecture is as distinctively English as Wedgwood pottery or Chippendale furniture, and boasts a much longer and more English descent.

The stone walls that over wide spaces take the place of hedgerows are of a piece with the rest; but breadth of outlook is so much a part of the glory of Cotswold that the imagination of pilgrims may regret the disappearance of days when sheep needed no enclosing and the wold seemed indeed without end. There is a famous signpost which directs you 'to the top of the world'; and the top of the world should have no boundaries. A signpost can be a part of the scenery, like a pylon or telegraph post or a bridge; and the number has been infinitely multiplied of late by the action of some county councils which have placarded every acknowledged pathway. They may add to the sentiment of the scene, as with such bold, simple notices as 'To the North' which decorate approaches to the Great North Road. Perhaps the most suggestive of all was a signpost outside one of the newest garden cities. It pointed towards Hatfield and bore the legend, 'The Way to Yesterday.' Most famous of all, at least in the eyes of visitors from the United States, directs travellers to York, Boston and Lincoln.

Cotswold is, of course, a watershed. It rises to a thousand feet, which is a great height in England, and extends for over sixty miles, which is a long distance in the scale of

English measurements. Its twenty-five miles or so of breadth provide a plain which might give the impression almost of aridity if it were not for the green grass which has been claimed as one of its most essential attributes. At any rate, on the wold one may forget the rivers; and their sudden appearance below a ridge is sometimes almost startling. It is partly the note of surprise that gives a certain eminence to the first view of Burford from above. You look down the long beautiful street to the Windrush at the bottom and seem to have opened a door into a new land. The Coln adds as much to Bibury as the Windrush to Burford. Both are comely streams, inviting the presence of houses at many points, but chiefly when they begin to reach the lower parts of the slope and make a scenic bond between upland and lowland. You may scarcely find two rivers in England quite like one another. The streams that ooze out of the chalk of the Chilterns—the Kennet and the Lea—have little likeness to the oolite streams—Coln, Windrush or the Thames itself. They travel, as a rule, wider valleys or at least less abrupt valleys—often wandering, as the Lea especially wanders, rather because there is an indecisive reason for one channel rather than another. The Cotswold rivers wind in direct obedience to decisive orders from the hills. How little likeness has either with the Severn, whose glorious junction with the Avon at Tewkesbury can be seen from the ridge! As little likeness have the Tudor houses that begin on the Tewkesbury plain with the stone Cotswold hamlets, or the upland wall with the midland hedge.

Perhaps the views over the west midland plains are the most ample; but the views from Cleeve Hill, which is the

highest point of the Cotswolds, are richer. It is difficult not
to give some special eminence to Stanway, whether you see
it from above or from almost any part of the road that runs
diagonally down the slope. It is characteristic of many road
views in England. Dwellers in great country houses with
wide parks had a habit of planting the edge of the park with
a broad band of deciduous trees. Whether you look at such
bands making a wall on one side or through such bands (as
by Haslemere), they 'half reveal and half conceal' what is
behind them, adding colour and mystery. The Stanway
road has unusually magnificent trees on the upper side,
which are a changing pageant as the seasons progress. On
the lower side the plain stretches out very green at all seasons
of the year, and at every step the panorama changes. The
golden moment of the view is in early autumn when the
first frosts have coloured the horse chestnuts and just
browned the beeches.

Plate 14. A stone village nestling in the hills,
Castle Combe

CHAPTER VI

The Hampshire Vale

The Weald is not the only interruption to the chalk along the eastern part of the south coast. The Hampshire Basin, so called, is no Weald to deserve an exclusive title, but it demands definition and nurses much that belongs most properly to the tale of the landscape that our people have created on the unseen vertebrae of the rocks.

A great German historian once wrote that you could not understand England and the English till you had read Gilbert White's *Selborne*. Now he has made immortal all parts of the scenery belonging to that pleasant Hampshire village; the 'Hanger' is a familiar thing in our literature and the ridge of the chalk hill behind is described in terms that have made it a locus classicus. To him the modest ridge was a magnificent mountain; and though it is not forbidden to laugh at the judgment, he is right. The archaeology, the scenery and the natural history of the parish all consent to a mutual relation in his pages; and his way of looking at a bit of England is the only way. Landscape is history in a picture as well as geology in a picture; and Hampshire is full of visible history through and through and across the sound into the Isle of Wight. The history is often as conspicuous as the coloured sands and tilted strata of the western end of that delectable island in the neighbourhood of the Needles.

Most visitors who approach Hampshire by land enter from the north over the downs; and no declivity in the land is more peaceful than the long valley which begins near Alton and ends at the coast. Its charm lies greatly in the mere greenness and the numbers of trees in clumps, in lines and in single glory. The road that follows the river just misses Selborne. Gilbert White, its scholar-parson in the latter part of the eighteenth century, was a pioneer in local archaeology and topography, as well as in natural history. All the world may know Selborne by heart; and the place is worthy of a universal acquaintance. Those who visit it in May have much ado to drag themselves away: they have found a paradise where hill and village embrace almost everything that is most proper to the scenery of southern England. They say that Gilbert White made Selborne immortal. It is true, but Selborne had a hand in making Gilbert White immortal. He was subdued to that he worked in. His mind was dipped in the dyes of Selborne itself. If the setting is of comparable value with the gem, Selborne may be hailed as peer to the loveliest English villages, even though the whole of the Cotswolds—with Bibury, Chipping Campden, Broadway, Stow-on-the-Wold and Bourton-on-the-Water—even though all our favourites, Elmley Castle, Compton Chamberlayne and Weobley, are entered for the competition.

English scenery owes much to the chalk, though Gilpin a century and a half ago held that the downs were repellent, were ugly without qualification. The South Downs with their firm lines and sweet grass and chattering wheatears are in their way incomparable, but we are aware of the greatest beauties when we have 'one foot on sea and one on shore', when we pass from the larger down and move seawards. Selborne has the qualities that belong to both hill and vale; and other virtues in the soil evoke the true gifts of the chalk. It favours two trees above others, the beech and the yew; and up the slope of that Hanger (which was almost an *alter ego* to White) you see aspects of the beech rare in other places. Up the slope and about the Zig-zag the beeches nurse one another into an 'O altitudo', as Sir Thomas Browne would have said. As the slope flattens into a table-land, single beech trees expand into the canopied pillar we are all familiar with. One reason why the beech is so splen-did in figure is that it allows no undergrowth. A beech wood is an aisle and transept without pews and other obstructions. The columns are seen for what they are and have this superiority over pillars, that the pedestal is organic and is decorated with its own gradations and flutings. They do not suffer undergrowth as kindly as the immense yew in the churchyard endures the rustic seat about it.

The beech grove is splendid, but the place is too hospi-table to permit of a monopoly. While on one side of the path, you mark the usual absence of small things under the massed beech trees, on the other the most apparent marvel is the groundwork of seedlings from ash and sycamore and other trees. They proclaim the congenial soil and clime. The bluff of the Hanger (and the watchfulness of the National Trust) encourages them. The whole region is clothed with trees, single and in groups and in woods by natural compulsion. And tinier things are germane to the

Plate 15. In the New Forest, Hampshire

ground thereabouts, not least the wood sorrel, whose leaves are more shapely and delicate than clover or shamrock, and the sanicle, most fastidious of its kind. In few places do the wild roses grow into such bold curves.

A place so commingled of wood and glade, of tree and undergrowth, of hill and valley, of shelter and freshness, must needs be a paradise of birds; and not even his archae/ ology, his topography, his tree or his tortoise delighted Gil/ bert White as the birds delighted him. His very words are winged: they rise to a music quite absent from some of the letters when he writes of the wood wren or even the rook and starling. He was always the scholar, often the man of science. He was only the poet when he heard the songs of birds. His birds are safe for their favourite part of the hill is a sanctuary, though anyone may walk there, for it belongs to the National Trust, and is preserved in perpetuity, an in/ violable fragment. The neighbourhood, like parts of Nor/ folk, creates naturalists, though the birds of Hants be/ long to the villages and of Norfolk to the wild. When you begin to descend from the South Downs (where the wheatears scuttle about like mice in the neighbourhood of their buried nests) and travel along the Meon valley all conditions prevail that give most of the small birds and many plants the ideal that they seek. They like trees to sing in and the lowest scrub to nest in, resembling the lark, though their aspiration is lower, in their fidelity to 'the kin/ dred points of heaven and home'. Yet they do not like woods. Trees that always avoid the dark density of woods are one mark of this region; and under their lee flourish those low shrubs and plants that the warblers best love. The

chiffchaff playing the cicada in the trees looks down on the
green roof over her nesting home. Some of the humbler
houses near the foot of the Hanger are almost like nests, so
hung-over are they by boughs, so persuasively inset after the
fashion that Morland painted.

Gilbert White's village and the valley of the Meon, by
which you descend upon Portsmouth, is to the east of the
Hampshire basin that has some close geological resem-
blance to the London basin, but the likeness is below the
surface. The Solent is no Thames. Hampshire has a nearer
likeness in some eyes to Norfolk, for the two counties are
famous among naturalists for the number and variety of
small birds, and among sportsmen as the favourite haunt of
that popular bird the partridge, which belongs essentially to
well-farmed land. The tree belts planted in most cases by
sportsmen greatly influence the scenery of Norfolk; but it
was another sort of hunter whose interests have retained for
Hampshire its most famous scene. The New Forest, as it
has been called for the last six hundred years, still holds up
its historical claims, though parts of it are the most popular
resort of tourists within the island, and a few of its glades
are no better than motor parks. The old names of its
governance survive. The Verderers' Court is in being for
better reasons than in the Forest of Dean, from which the
deer have now been wholly banished—and still from the
midst of the forest red deer rise before the wanderer. Still
they are hunted, but with horse and hound and no more
lethal weapon. That a hunting ground exclusively and
brutally preserved by early kings has become a popular
pleasure ground, has made amazingly little difference to the

general character of the scene. The beauty of many parts of the woodland is untarnished and the more open heaths retain their wildness. The greatest innovator has been the official afforester. Once when Buckler's Hard—that old descriptive noun for a deep place—was a great shipbuilding centre and England was defended by wooden walls, oaks were cultivated above other trees in and about the New Forest. When airplanes were invented some little scenes were quite altered by the planting of ash trees, whose tough and supple wood was more useful than the stubborn oak. Much at the same time the land was coveted by official afforesters and a good deal of damage done to this scene, as in Norfolk and Suffolk and Westmorland, by the excessive planting of too well regimented conifers. Nevertheless almost every well known and less well known place in the New Forest is lovely with glade and woodland or heath. Some of the beech trees are a landscape in themselves, but it is the variety of growth and alternation of woodland and open space that distinguish the whole district. Lyndhurst, Lymington, Brockenhurst, Beaulieu—it does not matter much where you go. The woodland roads are supreme, though as always you must obey Richard Jefferies' advice and 'get over the stile' to taste the finer quality; and even the most brutal motor driver must suppress his mania for speed. If the compulsion of the beauty does not influence him, he knows that a wild pony or even a red deer may cross his path at any moment.

Beaulieu, of course, is very different from the rest. The remains of the vast old Abbey dominate the scene, though the stones that remain are few. And the river plays a larger part in the scenery than in other New Forest villages. The trees themselves thereabouts suggest history; and they include that alien rarity, the deciduous cypress. Even the sport of the great landlords is conditioned by the landscape and has a scenic quality of its own. Sportsmen and beaters advance in line along either side of long shafts of woodland flanked by bracken, heather or whatnot. As the birds reach the end of their domain and must face either open land or the sea, they curl back over the heads of the advancing line. However hostile to the humane sense is the sound of gun or the baying of hounds, it is impossible to deny a strangely picturesque attribute in both the shooting of the woodcock and pheasant and the hunting of the deer in a New Forest scene. The hunting is the worse in spirit, but the more pleasing to the eyes that it is especially popular in springtime and in early autumn.

In the New Forest, if you avoid some of the more recent plantations of conifers you cannot find a place that does not appeal to the aesthetic sense, and often to the historic. The greatest of newspaper editors, by that date an octogenarian, wrote from Manchester to a dweller in the south to ask if he would find for him a particular great beech tree growing near Lyndhurst. The splendid thing, with its wide canopy of boughs, as shapely in winter as green in spring, the dome above and the smooth grey masterful trunk had stayed in his mind irremovably; and he longed in his old age to repeat the delight that filled him when first he saw it in his middle age. Such magnificent trees there are; but there are greater elsewhere—by High Wycombe and in Savernake, for example. It is the woodland itself and the spaces between the groves and the trees themselves that make the New Forest a great national resort.

There are one or two gardens belonging to country houses that are a landscape in themselves, streams and trees and hills and valleys. All the gardening is by natural compulsion landscape gardening, a form of the art in which England was a pioneer and has long excelled. The pergolas leading to the wood at Gravetye in Sussex are but a development of John Evelyn's famous holly hedge. If one had to pick the spot most eloquent of history, Buckler's Hard would come second only to Beaulieu. It is unparalleled, too, in its present guise as in its industrial history. It was once the most famous of all shipping yards. The quaint, broad, straight but very short street runs down to the Hard, the deep place on the river, that was the cause of its selection. The river is still bright with shipping that becomes a part of the landscape as in the Norfolk Broads. The New Forest in its essential form is to the north, but southwards towards the sea edge is a wild resort of duck and wading birds who find their perfect sum of conditions in marsh and inlet.

Most of the New Forest lies west and north-west of Southampton Water on the way to Bournemouth, which may be called the king of modern towns, where at last the fir and pine are truly native. It leads towards the iron sands and heaths of Dorset. The other side of Southampton Water and of Portsmouth is richer and tamer; and at Cosham and Bosham, the strawberry plant is more in evidence than the beech and oak.

The New Forest was lucky enough to escape the fate of a

similar region, of some 700,000 acres, a little further to the west. It was not disafforested, like Cranborne Chase. A forest was the hunting ground of a king; a chase the hunting ground of a lesser personage; but it was not its lack of royal status that condemned Cranborne, which varied at different ages from a chase to a forest to a chase. It became a haunt of bands of undesirable persons; and since it fell out of its repute as a sanctuary for deer in the middle of the nineteenth century, its wilder glories have departed. The Cerne Abbas Giant looks down on smiling farms and well spaced trees. Yet the deer maintain their place, as in the New Forest; and the New Forest itself has no scene of rough splendour that surpasses the smaller untamed relic of the old chase in the neighbourhood of Stubhampton about halfway between Shaftesbury and Cranborne along the Wiltshire Border and east of the Blackmore Vale. The fame of Lulworth Cove and Corfe Castle and the coast in general had perhaps led to some neglect of inland Dorset till Thomas Hardy sent a horde of pilgrims to his Casterbridge and Egdon Heath.

Purbeck Isle, which has been described as Dorset in miniature, is known largely for its marble; and it is a suggestive commentary on the foundations of England that various sorts of strata have purely local names. In the Hampshire basin we meet again the Wealden clay. On the southern side of the basin, especially on the north coast of the Isle of Wight between Bembridge and Sea View, the 'blue slipper' clay—a very accurate local name—suggests the coast of Norfolk near Cromer, or the slopes inland of the plain of Rye. It is a treacherous soil, terribly inconstant

Plate 16. The windswept Downs of the Isle of Wight

whenever rain is excessive and the cliffs of it recede and re-cede leaving a clayey beach. Sometimes the wild clematis or traveller's joy, which not seldom climbs to the very tops of the trees, tumbles to the shore with the clay and even there grows well enough to hide the debris.

Hampshire, since most of it occupies a breach in the chalk, has the virtue of down and vale. It is various but very distinct in character like Kent. It, too, is a garden of England, and if there were voting for the loveliest county, it would come high.

England possesses a number of harbours made lovely by the land that shelters them. Falmouth, one of the most land-lovely, if one may say so, and Plymouth Hoe need no bush. Of them all, Southampton Water is most like a lake. It belongs to the land as the South Downs belong to the sea. You steam among the houses by the glades of the forest.

The Isle of Wight gets its name perhaps from the same placard as Albion itself, for the Culver cliffs and the Needles (which are one fewer than they were two centuries ago) are white as the Dover cliffs. They are rims of the basin, as are the South Downs. The isle is most English, but has some views and attributes very rare in England. The trees come down to the water's edge, whereas in less serene places, the winds are too salt and rough for trees, which dare approach it only in snug valleys such as Lee and Lynmouth in North Devon. Oaks grow to a fair size within twenty yards of the high tide mark on the eastern outskirts of Ryde and conifers drop their cones in the salt water to the west. Few views are more constantly changeable according to the shifts of the weather and the hour of the day than the

F

prospect across the sound from the steep acclivity above the northern shore. The low slopes behind Portsmouth and Southsea and the high downs behind them appear and disʹ appear in such variety of gradation that the prospect is daily, is hourly new; and the tides add to the transformation. At the lowest they leave a stretch of sand a mile or so in width. At their highest they pound against the sea wall and sea walk raised to arrest them. The tides here and on both sides of the Channel are great makers of scenery. The sea runs in from the west like a rapid river. You may watch its motion almost as clearly as the boiling tide between Ramsey Island and the mainland just south of St. David's Head. It was perhaps the sight of this stream, so fast at one hour, so still in the next, that suggested to Tennyson the best line of his popular poem, *Crossing the Bar*. 'Too full for sound or foam.' He did not live in the Isle of Wight for nothing and you may trace most characteristics of its scenery (including the trees at the sea's edge) in isolated pictorial lines. Robert Bridges is hardly more eloquent of the Berkshire Thames and its buttercup meadows, where the cows are said to rob the golden market of the bees. They do, in the sense that you may see their bellies yellowed by the pollen of the flowers that no beast eats.

The lover of scenery will see a certain likeness between the Weald and the Hampshire basin; but they are contrary in the view of the geologist. The Weald was made by the wearing away of lifted strata, the Hampshire basin repreʹ sents a real dip and has its true analogy in the London basin. In the Isle of Wight, the central ridge of chalk, that is the nucleus of the diamond shape of the island, is much

less well known than the seaside places: the harbours of
Bembridge, Ryde and Cowes, the popular holiday haunts
of Seaview, Ventnor, Shanklin and the neighbourhood of
Tennyson's house at 'the Needles end'. But the ridge itself
has individual qualities and hides many lovely nooks of
which perhaps the pride is Appuldurcombe. The ridge
partakes of the nature of the South Downs.

CHAPTER VII

The Shires

The Midlands are not regarded as among the more beautiful parts of England. They are hardly a golden mean,
an *aurea mediocritas*; but they are intensely English; and
though the term is vague topographically, there is a very definite Midland quality in the scenery both as made by
nature and as made by man.

As you leave the lowland fens and marshes you rise slowly on clay slopes; and absurdly low though the absolute
altitude is, the width of view may be magnificent. One may
be allowed to claim that the essential Midland quality of
scene and soil, of farm and village, begins with the Great
North Road between Huntingdon and Peterboro'. The
key point is the top of a hill rising from the village of Alconbury to the almost vanished village of Stilton, a name
famous among epicures. Looking east from an observation
post close to the main road, you have a view as wide as the
prospect from Ivinghoe Beacon; but it is a panorama of
just space and colour. The soft haze that belongs to the Fens
is over it; and though you may map out some landmarks,
none leaps to the eye. You might almost be looking over the
sea. Direction posts for motorists bear the short legend, 'To
the North', as if no one would dream of pausing in the
middle piece.

The country west of the Great North Road south of

84

Peterboro' bears the marks of its own shrinkage. It is a land of little towns, of little villages, of little woods and spinneys. Even the counties are small. Huntingdon and Rutland are also empty. For a number of generations the census has shown a falling off of the population; and what happens to the denizens is always expressed in the scenery. The land is greener, for grass has succeeded to tilth. The splendid churches look more and more supreme over the little hamlets about them. A diminution of wealth in the squires and landowners is told by the substitution of corrugated iron for thatch. Some cottages have been left to crumble into ruins, like the houses, may one say, of deserted mining camps.

A very true bit of the scenery of these eastern Midlands is familiar to many pilgrims who have made their way to Little Gidding. It was a very flourishing place in the reign of Charles I, when the Farrars kept their religious home there, and worshipped in the little chapel. Shorthouse's description in *John Inglesant* brought many visitors to this quiet place. Old avenues and a succession of monkish fish ponds lead down the hill towards the slow winding brook and past a gorse of a few acres which is as famous among the hunting community as the chapel among historians. Great Gidding on the other side has dwindled in a generation from a population of 800 to a still dwindling population of about 200; and the hill looks down on a magnificent tower 'rising from a grove of elms' and a village of about 120 souls. The glebe contains a moat and mounds that were foundations of fine houses, all indicating that the place was busy and populous before the Reformation, probably long before.

Plate 17. The agricultural landscape of Rutland

One may say that all except their sport is fled; for those grass fields and quick hedges and compact woods have given the hunt ideal conditions. Foxhunting is the chief industry, outside farming, and horse and hound bring the country its brightest days of spectacular merriment. The sport itself has influenced the scenery in small details. Just as the sport of shooting has encouraged in Norfolk the numberless belts of fir, so hunting has helped to maintain the hedgerow against its rival, the wire fence. Such influence is more direct and positive and general when you reach the heart of the Midlands and the famous hunting counties of Leicester and Northampton.

Now the hedgerow is perhaps the most distinctive of all the marks on the surface of this England. With the stone wall of the north and the mud walls of the west, it patterns out the greater part of the surface of the land. Visitors from overseas, and above all those who get a bird'seye view of the land from an airplane, speak with admiring wonder of the little closes and homelike neatness of field and paddock. It looks to them to be a land composed of gardens and houses. It is the hedgerow that makes this effect general, as any flight in the air will make plain. So carefully pencilled out is all the land that you see the affectionate touch of Englishmen in every yard of England, where hedges prevail.

Writers on scenery landscape begin as a rule with geology, on the plausible theory that the bones matter more than the flesh. Yet the geology of England remains more or less constant: the scenery has altered profoundly within years too few to be reckoned in terms of geological time. The hedge is a new thing, in its general extension. The Saxon village was surrounded by a hedge, and the deer-parks were 'ribbed and paled in' as soon as the democratic threats began, and the swineherd desired to feed his pigs in woods that were wanted for the hunt. Such hedges were rare and few till the era of enclosures; and perhaps did not become integral to British scenery as we know it till the second great wave of enclosure towards the middle of the eighteenth century. The earlier enclosures were made chiefly on behalf of the wool merchants, and sheep need wide pastures. Later enclosures were rather for the sake of arable farming, wheat was in greater demand than wool and the defence of the crop against marauding animals must be thorough. So we find that precise and yet more precise regulations were enforced as to fencing off the enclosed fields. The ditches must be just so deep, just so wide at the top and just so much narrower at the bottom. The parapet was to be set with bushes of quick-thorn after a particular model. May or quick or hawthorn was the master plant of the countryside from early days. It encircled, as is probable, with interpolated blackthorn, the Saxon village. It was familiar to the first shepherds: they told their tale

Under the hawthorn in the dale.

In the eighteenth century it ruled out England into small and kindly paddocks or closes, from which or into which no animal could stray. Within the shelter of the quicks, seeds of all sorts found protection and the rising suckers of elm and blackberry or briar were safe from the knife. In the early days no roads were hedged or fenced. It was indeed recognised as a traveller's right to voyage along the field when the sunk and unmetalled road became too foul; and 'ways were foul' with a vengeance. Then the new farming and the new transport compelled the fencing of the roads, and the full domesticity of the landscape was proclaimed. A rough, forbidding country of forest and scrub and marsh grew into the likeness of a garden or a homestead. Even to-day in an urban and suburban world hedging and ditching remain as essential rural crafts.

The hedge matters most, both for farmer and aesthete in the Midlands, where specific names have been coined, such as the 'oxer', the 'double oxer' and the 'bullfinch'. After the Great War was over expert hedgers became lamentably few, and the neglect of the ditches left many fields so water-logged that they fell out of cultivation. In this crisis it was found that the art of hedging survived in its perfection only, or at least chiefly, in Leicestershire, which is by general con-fession the core of the Midlands. There the technique of hedging had been essentially influenced by the hunts, which demand a barrier that could be leaped without un-necessary danger. The stakes of 'laid' hedges were not to project above the wattle; and so it may be claimed that the fox hunter of our days, as the stag hunter of the fifteenth century, definitely affected the nature of the scenery. The hedge-laying experts from Leicestershire were sent as mis-sionaries to many counties; and some of their most ardent pupils in this matter of scene-painting were found among unemployed factory hands, some of whom plied their new craft up to the very edges of the great towns, not least in Essex.

England's gems of scenery are not found in the Midlands; but a particular beauty of colour and form invests the rich green grass fields of the shires of Leicester, Northampton or Rutland round about the most famous kennels of foxhounds. A level land consisting for the most part of heavy clay has changed from a waste of bog and forest into a green and pleasant land, dotted with broad towns and fair villages. The villages, in spite of 'ribbon development', keep the homely beauty that the bigger towns have rejected.

If the Midlands are the one part of England against which a certain monotony may be alleged, they are nevertheless freely sprinkled with surprises and sudden beauties. The strange sandhill that gives Sandy its name and provides the market gardeners of Bedford with their optimum of conditions may be quoted though it is not within the Midlands proper. The most startling, to the geologist as to the observer of surface scenery, is undoubtedly Charnwood Forest. It would be difficult to find a near parallel. It is to the people of Leicester what the Peak of Derbyshire is to a great group of north Midland towns.

We all know that the word forest does not necessarily connote dense woodland or even sparse woodland. Some of the barest surfaces in the north belong to deer forests. Clun Forest and Radnor Forest, though Clun has plentiful trees on the valley side, consist of upland wastes where trees, or none or few, find a foothold. Charnwood, as many existing signs convince, was once a woodland forest denser perhaps over a wider space than any single forest in the land. It stretched from the Warwickshire forest of Arden almost to Derby. Several old descriptions of it are extant, indicating the continuous density of the trees. A squirrel could travel a score of miles without touching the ground; a man could travel as far without seeing the sun. Here and there the rocks come out on the surface and must always have been free from trees. These are to-day favourite 'gazebos', in the artificial tongue of eighteenth century nature-fakers, and consist of a few peaks of protruding stone, approached either by grass roads or by tussocks of grass as deep and spongy as on the island of Grassholm where the gannets nest on rock flanked by mounds of 'Yorkshire fog'. Below the peaks narrow woods, chiefly of beech and oak, wind their way between cultivated fields, chiefly of grass.

The protruding stones indicate the miracle of Charnwood. The upland consists of a sudden uprising of granite from the clayey plain. Like the Malvern Hills, which have survived in erect form because their core is hard, the stone has attracted the quarryman. The walls of the quarries suggest the defences of some giant city of myth; and somehow they do not offend the eye in Charnwood as they may in some parts of the Malverns. They may be almost called splendid, after their fashion, especially when first seen through intervening trees. The scale of the quarrying, not least at Mount Sorel, is immense. The stone is loosened, is felled by explosives, and one of the major operations gives the effect of some great natural commotion of volcanic origin. The side of the hill moves forward with what appears to be extreme deliberation before the force of the explosion 'topples the topmost towers of Ilium'. The solid moving mass crashes in utter ruin while the noise of the released dynamite booms like thunder. In this way, too, man makes his scenery. There are sandhills—as at Codicote in Hertfordshire—which have as good as vanished. The hill itself has been dug up, has been carted away. In the slate districts of Wales, as near Llanberis under Snowdon, the gorse-clad hill has been converted into a forbidding wall, grim yet not altogether without its own beauty. Here and there tarns have been formed below the flattened wall, and standing at the edge you may well be reminded of those best of Tennysonian descriptions:

Like night dews on still waters between walls
Of shadowy granite in a gleaming pass.

Slate is not granite nor as beautiful; but the comparison will serve. None of these landscape removals is more salient than the Charnwood quarries, which proclaim the foundations of this gracious upland, not less surely and much more scenically than the wide clay pits round about Peterboro', where Huntington, Northampton and Lincoln join, or the deeper pits of Arlesey, in Bedfordshire, pointing the contrast to the sudden sandhill of Sandy.

From whatever side you approach Charnwood the sharp contrast is impressed on you. Coventry and Coalville, which is indeed a town of coal, make an almost continuous forest of houses. Leicester, a town of very different sort, and very characteristic of the straightforward plan of the Midlands, is close up to the edge of the rise. The contrast between the Forest and Quorndon is hardly less abrupt, though you do not pass from the urban to the rural. Quorndon is famous in the annals of the sport of which the shires are peculiarly proud. It may be called the headquarters of fox-

hunting in its modern sense; and has claims of more historical worth than even Belvoir, where a trio of noble lords
met to found the first of the organised hunts, or than Melton
Mowbray whose dudes at a little later date were notorious
for their contempt of the provincials. Quorndon is a very
comely village 'of the lawn', and 'of the plain' like Oliver
Goldsmith's 'Sweet Auburn', but it begins to climb the
quick ascent from clay to granite. It was in Lincolnshire
not Leicestershire that a political Master of Foxhounds was
asked by a heckler what was the chief industry of his parts.
He wisely and truly replied with emphasis, 'Fox 'untin'.' The
answer would be yet truer of Quorndon. It is a curious fact
that the villages which are hunting headquarters are more
carefully manicured, if the word be forgiven, than most
other villages. Some not very kindly things have been said
of the lovely village of Broadway, since its fame about the
world, especially in the books of American touring agen-
cies, has made it a little self-conscious even in facial expres-
sion. But the tidiness and comfortable richness of Broadway yield to the trim wealth of Quorndon, and Quorndon
itself is exceeded by Waddesdon, which in some regards it
resembles in spite of the differences between the shires of
Buckinghamshire and Leicester.

From Quorndon, where the fast and plutocratic hunt
was perfected, the road rises steeply to the most distinctive
area of the Charnwood plateau. First come neat and quaint
mounds crowned, one by trees, another by a windmill, too
picturesque to be useful. You have the impression as you
mount the slope, of a forest that refuses to be exterminated.
Trees well spaced along the hedgerows are one of the most

Plate 18. Hunting country; a Meet at Melton Mowbray

characteristic decorations of the English scene. They are beautiful and gloriously useless, if not harmful. Hereabouts hedgerow timber is more continuous than continual. Now and again the trees are the hedge. Little bits of woodland crop up, like the granite itself, at quite illogical distances. Even birch plantations are to be found. As you pass to the top of the acclivity through such scenes as these irrepressible trees compose, you reach Copt Oak, which was once the headquarters of the government of the forest, when it was a forest indeed. It is now an oakless crossroads, and one of the least remarkable spots within the circle of the forest, retaining none of the beauties or palpable historic charm of the speech-house in the Forest of Dean or the Verderers' halls of either Epping or the New Forest. Yet once there you have the freedom of the forest: and a gracious landscape of green fields and groves and stony pinnacles and bits of forest open before you whichever way you move. The Midland plain, with its oxers and double oxers, its most jumpable brooks, its rich flat grazing fields, seems as far off as the industrial and manufacturing towns or the coal-mining townships.

Nottingham, like Leicester, is an amalgam of mines and husbandry; it is difficult as you travel across it to think of it in terms of the Robin Hood romance. But Sherwood Forest, made wild by the sand and gravel of the subsoil, has noble relics of the days before the forest was cleared, or 'the Dukeries' came into being. Of the immense forest enclosed in the sixteenth century by one of the biggest of those revolutionary acts, seven or eight remain untamed and there are oaks older than the myth of Little John. Someone called

the Trent 'a very Midland river'; but the country north of it
is more northern than Midland. The great plain of York
juts well into it and the Peak of Derbyshire is a visible
neighbour.

It would be of no service, if it were possible, to define the
Midlands, or even 'the Shires'. Leicester and Northampton come first to the mind; but it has been said that Stratford-on-Avon is the middle of England physically as well
as spiritually. There lived the man who found the best
epithet in literature for our island: '*This* England,' a place
always close to us, palpable and homely, where every man
has something English within sight of his window, within
reach of his finger tips.

When you descend from the wolds you know for sure
that you are in the Midlands, though they will become
plainer as you move north. The Avon is a river rather of the
plain than the valley, though not less lovely on that account.
At Stratford it is crossed by one of the lovelier bridges of
England. One may perhaps compare it in its scenic quality
with the bridge over the Ouse between Huntingdon and
Godmanchester. When the river passes through the arches
it becomes Shakespeare's river. All the approaches to Stratford, except the Warwick road, have lost all historic flavour,
all modern charm. This road, roughly parallel with the
river and a green well-treed bank, still savours of Shakespeare. It is English to the core and some of the farms and
villages and separate houses survive in an unspoilt setting.
Snitterfield—a most English name—is a Shakespearean
village still, in spite of regrettable additions. As you approach Warwick, as you pass under the old entrance gates

you may still taste the Shakespeare of *Richard II* as you have tasted the Shakespeare of *As You Like It* or the *Midsummer Night's Dream*. The views of the castle are compact of history. You are nearer the forest of Arden and the home of the king-maker than of the Black Country, though that is closely juxtaposed.

We use the word 'black' in several senses. There are two ranges of Black Mountains, and the name is as true a compliment to the depths of their shadow as was paid to the Black Forest in Germany. The Black Country is not a term of praise though many fair fields and villages and a host of fair houses are in it. Birmingham overrides parts of Warwickshire as completely as William Cobbett found 'the Wen' to deface Surrey and Essex. Some of its influences are strange and unexpected. Many a fine crop of wheat in its neighbourhood has been winnowed by the hordes of sparrows that make a practice of emigrating from the town for their August holiday in the country. They may be said to have altered the landscape by their influence in encouraging the shift from arable land to grass, so that Warwickshire comes into line in this regard with Leicester and Northampton. If any part of England is uniform, the Midlands are uniform here as we have seen in other counties, but you never know when a wood or spinney will not transform the landscape. In the plain and humdrum county of Huntingdon, how fair a succession of sights passes before the rider to hounds who is taken from Monks Wood to Aversley, to Gidding Gorse, to Hamerton Grove, to Salome and Buckworth Woods. The follower of the Woodland Pytchley in the very centre of the shires is checked by

larger woods—if Monks Wood be excepted—and each has
its own character, as their generic titles often imply. Grove
and gorse and wood and spinney and wold succeed one
another, strung out in a varied chain. The 'rides' of the
bigger woods deserve a special paean. Some were made for
the sake of sport; and they are useful both to the follower of
the hunt and man with the gun; but they suggest rather the
cloister of a sanctuary. The walls are frescoed with the
coloured pattern of many bushes and the trees suggest the
architectural column, as in any avenue. They are the playground of all the animals in the wood; and many flowers
desiring more light than the central wood offers creep up to
their edge. If England were merely a thing of hills and
valleys, of ups and downs, of chasm and precipice and
rushing river and great lakes, of spacious views enhanced
by the telescope, then the Midlands would be dull enough;
but the glory of England is not telescopic: it is close, intimate, belonging more to the naturalist than the geologist,
more to the saunterer (if saunter is derived from *sainte terre*,
as Thoreau imagined) than to the geographer. By this
definition there are few parishes in middle England that
are short of charm.

A rich history adds to their attractions. The most solitary
hamlets have held large populations. H. L. Fisher, greatest
of our historians, has given the evidence for believing that
in the country round about Gray's churchyard in Bucks,
the population has steadily dwindled since the days of
Elizabeth. The fight with the forests moved slowly forward, we may imagine, from east to west; and the chalk
and perhaps the clay country gave hospitality to a busy

population while yet the hills of the west were a dreaded hinterland of mystery. The geology of the west is old, even in relation to the structure of the continent. The surface of the east is new; but the civilisation, one may say, is in in-verse ratio to the antiquity of the rocks. The plough made a very slow progress from Dover to Holyhead. It has been claimed that the English language itself, as we speak it, spread from the monasteries on the Nene, and 'Middle En-glish' is a proper product of Northamptonshire. The Mid-lands are middle England in many senses, and partake fully of its aesthetic qualities.

CHAPTER VIII

The South-West Peninsula

The types of landscape in this England do not follow county boundaries. Hills and downs, rivers and forests run our artificial distinctions together; and it is hard to say with any exactitude where hills and downs themselves begin or end. Wiltshire partakes of Berkshire, Sussex of Hampshire, Huntingdon of Cambridge and Northampton and Westmorland of Cumberland. If there is any exception to the rule it is in the 'toe' of England. Cornwall and Devon, though famous rivals of one another and very different in many regards, partake little of other counties. Each, like Corinth, faces two seas, each is *bimaris*. Each has nooks where the climate may be called sub-tropical. So rare is hard frost and so soft the air, even in days of tempest you would hardly suspect this quality in Cornwall when you stand on the ridge. The wind carrying salt on its blast sheers trees almost to extinction. Wherever a group are collected for protection they slope towards the sea, the lowest nearest. Even at the back the tree is a low and stunted thing that might have come from the pages of Doré's *Purgatory*. One ingenious topographer went in search of a grove that bridged the ridge and so shaped both ways; planed by the Channel winds on one side and the Atlantic on the other. The old Saxon village, unearthed in this generation, on the ridge above Penzance, has no protection from any tree; and

98

Plate 19. The Exmoor Hills, looking towards Porlock

seems strangely placed when we think of our snug comfortable villages strung along the streams of inland valleys.
Our predecessors had a greater fondness for stark heights
than we have. Roman roads and much earlier roads run
along crests, like the Ridgeway and others that are now
scarcely traceable (except, perhaps, by the greater number of
daisies that flourish on the hardened bed). The great camps
were on the hills, a thing easy to understand, except for the
wonder how the folk and the flocks fared for water, that
necessity of life which has peopled the valleys of the world.
Few places are bleaker than parts of the Cornish ridge; and
a full allowance of grimness has been imparted to the landscape by the mines, the strange heaps of white from the
china clay diggings as well as mounds from the tin mines.
Minerals play a considerable part in the landscape. The
granite basis announces itself in outcrops and starves the
herbage; the immensely solid gate-posts, popular over much
of the west country, sparkle strangely with mica. So sparkle,
but more oddly, many ploughed fields in the home
counties, but in these the sun catches atoms of the glass that
is included in most of the manure collected in London.

If it were not that pleasure in wildness increases as civilisation grows tamer, we might find a good part of Cornwall
lonely and grim, yet few counties have more snug and
comely nooks. Tender spring flowers and vegetables find
their ideal environment above the granite. Daffodils are
grown in wide enough fields to be called a part of the
landscape. Only in bits of land torn off from Cornwall by
the Atlantic are spring flowers more successfully grown;
and the Scillies are Cornish in almost all respects. Only in

Cornwall is the spring broccoli grown in quantity and quickly enough to supply an export trade. In no country within the island does the smallholder flourish so regularly. One of the continual contrasts of east and west is that the village is in some measure supplanted by the homestead. Small cottage-like homesteads dot the landscape; and they are inhabited in Cornwall by a yeomanry of singular prosperity and pride both in their profession and their county. The climate is kindly to the tender cattle of the Channel Islands; and one may say that Jerseys and Guernseys look as if they were native. Much of the coast, both to the north and the south, is dangerous and forbidding enough; but this sudden surprising snugness and warmth is expressed even on the north coast in the lovely harbour of St. Ives, a famous centre for artists by mere reason of its scenic charm. To the south palm trees grow in Penzance; and all round the shores you might search in vain for such a well sheltered gem as the tiny harbour of Mouseholes. The famous St. Michael's Mount, that almost-island, is smaller and less salient than its counterpart Mont St. Michel in Brittany, but it is by comparison warm and homely, and a rock most agreeable to flowers. In spite of the exposure of the whole peninsula to the sea winds, the climate is too warm and genial for the wellbeing of some of the fruits that like a cold region. Apple growers complain that the trees 'never go to sleep'. They grow late in one year and early in the next, and the soft wood is never hardened off.

Wherever one is in Cornwall one thinks of the coast. Devon (in spite of Charles Kingsley and men of Bideford, in spite of its southern seaside resorts and its magnificent northern headlands) leaves a sense of deep inland seclusion. The Combe, one may say, matters most. All of us who have loved a county, a district, a country, nurse a particular scene that stands to us for the type. For example, there is a treeless slope, part of it national property, which looks down on the spacious sands of Woolacombe and over to the ruggedness of Morte Point. The one road up it is so steep that it is difficult to keep its surface firm enough for modern modes of motion. When you achieve the top and progress a very little further you are all of a sudden in another land, in mood singularly 'remote from the mutations and unrest' of the sea or the thought of it. A narrow valley richly treed on both sides is below you. A little trickling stream runs along the base. Buildings very old, and next to the buildings a very comfortable and domestic country house just appear from the grove. In spring patches of field and open wood are so thick with primroses that they influence the general scene. No rough winds blow, though flecks of foam from a tempestuous sea are carried over it. That is the very Devonshire. This inland nature in a county that is really part of a not very broad peninsula is sometimes expressed in nooks or combes that are organic parts of the seaside places. Lee is perhaps the best example. You must descend a very steep hill, however you approach it. Trees and grass of brilliant greenery and gardens of sub-tropical richness flank the roads. You hardly suspect the sea till you are at the tiny shore, or from a road nearer the coast catch a glimpse of blue waters through the trees. The cleft is warm and sheltered as an inglenook. You are almost indoors as well as inland. There is nothing quite like this in any other part of

England, though trees come even nearer the water's edge at a good many places, not least notably in that part of Hampshire which we call the Isle of Wight. There, too, the primroses are massed; but the infinitely steep well-clothed walls of the combe make all the difference. They shut out the world, even the sea itself; and break up the height of the land into a thousand surprises.

The lanes have often a queer likeness to the combes. They are close and warm, and nourish a lush growth which may on occasion stop your passage. The walls or cuttings are rock gardens in which bush and flower compete; and the bushes are apt to win if the lane is not shorn by the local farmer or authority.

The combe and the lane fill a large part of the remembered impression of Devon; but this is truer of north Devon than of south; and the division into north and south in popular speech is more real than such distinctions usually are. How unreal, for example, is the dichotomy of the Cotswolds and in some respect of the Yorkshire Ridings! When the Phoenicians sailed up the Dart into Totnes they saw, so far as the woods allowed them, a rich, rolling country, of wide aspect, desirable for quiet homes. The mouth of the Dart has some claims to be the loveliest river outflow in the island. The few buildings in the steeper rocks seem to be part and parcel of the cliff. Very quietly the bend that takes you within sight of the naval college, hides the sea. The wood just beyond is so well-treed that the thousands of homing rooks add a picture to the evening scene, so regular is their appearance, so large their company. The outlook is not without spaciousness as you advance

Plate 20. A Devonshire valley; East Lyn

inland to the favourite Phoenician landing place, passing at Dartington Hall one of the most English of country estates. It is now the scene of a great experiment in rural crafts and modern education. An imported style of archi-tecture, in which the flat roof prevails, has spread from there, and certainly not improved the prospect of a number of Devonshire points of beauty; but the native loveliness of house and park and well spaced trees has not been tarnished; and the increase of busy workers and their apparatus is all to the good even in the eyes of the mere aesthete. What a pleasure to the eyes, for example, is a waterwheel or a herd of Guernsey cattle; and the craft of forestry, though in large measure concerned with the reduction of live trunk to dead timber, may go hand in hand with nature in pleasant part-nership. Here, as we said elsewhere, nothing is more char-acteristic of England than the scattered trees that remain from the dense woodlands. They are treasured like historic monuments, especially if they are oaks, like the oaks of Hatfield, propped with crutches; or the hollowed trunks at Aldermaston in Berkshire, the veteran elm of Richmond Park or the yews of Christchurch. The Dart has given its name to its own birthplace; but Dartmoor and Exmoor are of such an individual character that they belong to their own scenic class. It is a tribute to the richness of Devon (a word more highly approved than Devonshire) that its in-land places, its coast and its moors all demand a special treatment.

It has been dogmatically stated that 'the West Country', a phrase which indicates a sort of unity, as of a place possessing more than a geographical bond, means Cornwall, Devon, Somerset and Dorset. Somerset is beyond dispute of the west, western. It is coupled with Devon in the name of the Devon and Somerset staghounds which pursue a quarry that belongs more naturally to the north-eastern end of Exmoor than to any other part of England. The most pictorial and biggest of all our mammals, the red deer, gloriously described in life and at its death by a member of a great Devon family, was routed from most parts of Britain by the plough and the farm. Nowhere, not even in the New Forest, does it so intimately belong to the landscape as along the north-western frontier of Somerset. Every pilgrim to England should make his way up to Exmoor and towards the north coast of Devon from the base of Dulverton and its neighbourhood. The junction of the rivers, where also trout and salmon and otter live, the groves of trees on the higher slopes above the river, the comely village half hidden in trees, the steep gradient to the moor in front compound a landscape rich in most qualities. It is wild and domestic, a sanctuary and a hunting ground, a Mecca and a posting inn. The geologists find strange variants, explaining the variety of scene with a directness rare in the rest of England. There is one point of view that tells all; and it is famous both in legend and history. Glastonbury Tor is not very high. You may walk up it in half an hour, and it has none of the grandeur of a mountain when you reach the tower at the peak. It is good grazing ground, not for deer but for domestic cattle. Its virtue is that the conical hill rises unaccompanied within a plain. If Joseph of Arimathea ever ascended it, as a sturdy legend maintains, he enjoyed that rarity in landscape, a

circular view. It is wide in all directions and in the light of
sunset 'mystic, wonderful' like the clothing of the arm that
received King Arthur's sword, when he had departed to
the island of Avalon. The view is widest towards the south
and west over the immense marsh or lake, as it once was,
where now the road runs between lines of willows. Little is
left of the monastery or of other relics of a greater antiquity,
but any pilgrim to Glastonbury will find his reward in the
prospect from the Tor. The romance of the scene is in-
destructible. It is wide enough to beautify the worst that
man can do. Very different is the outlook from the wooded
tor at Wells, whose crown of beauty is the cathedral itself,
that miniature medieval wonder, seen in the framework of
the trees before the peak of the hill is reached.

Not so many years ago, less than two hundred, a great
gulf was fixed between Devon and Somerset towards the
middle and the south. It was in the days when roads all
took the high land, avoiding both the mud and water or
thicket growth of the lowland, and missing the steeper
valleys cut by rivers. To-day the straightest and fastest roads
in the county run through the old marsh.

Now Somerset has famous flat lands and marshes as well
as hills and undulations. It has been argued in speech by a
great student of our husbandry that Somerset contains an
example of the very highest sort in every department of pro-
duction from the land, and he might have extended his
claim to what lies well below the surface, for the precious
stone, equally pleasing to the mason and artist, that is found
in the Mendips and Ham Hill, has encouraged the building of gracious houses and stately abbeys these thousand

years and more. Perhaps the husbandman was thinking of rich meadows that are the formal cause of cheddar cheese, of crops of roots and sugar-beet, of sheep on the uplands and such conventionally agricultural products; but the claim may be extended to rural crafts. One of these is basket work made of the willows and osiers that grow to perfection about the old marshes that once so severed Devon from her easterly neighbours that the easiest route was by sea. The marshes, progressively drained over a long period by native, not Dutch engineers, suggest the eastern Fens in some re-gards, chiefly in those lines of pollard willows along the roads, but the likeness is casual and partial. The meadow not the tilth is the prevailing feature. The greenness and the water, whether in stream or ditch, belong to the west not the east. However good all sorts of crops may be, Somerset is not essentially a granary. It is vividly green all the year round. Some reference books begin their description of it by announcing that Somerset is a maritime county. As with Devon, you forget that attribute as soon as you are out of sight of the sea; and a good part of the sea is cut off by some of the highest land in southern England; and the Bristol Channel seems little more than a river. Indeed, this bit of Britain defies the generalisation of any single adjec-tive more completely perhaps than any other county or shire. It has a great deal of what once was marsh, a great deal of hill and moor and wide spaces of rolling plain. It has caves and gorges and even islands, like those of the Fens. In the historic or half-historic spirit that they evoke, 'the Isle of Avalon' may compare with the Isle of Ely. That isle and Glastonbury Tor set the imagination throbbing before

they are seen, and the eyes do not disappoint—unless the
abbey is visited on a public holiday. That usually hideous
thing and always hideous name, a garage, is necessary at
any place that has fame or notoriety. It is impossible to keep
such holy places altogether 'unspotted from the world' as all
who visit Glastonbury or Wells Cathedral will know, yet
the glory has not passed away from the place or its name.
The holy thorn or winter-flowering variety of the quick,
flowers if not at Christmas yet at no long remove; and
green leaves and green blades protect the green thoughts
that belong to this romantic centre of 'England's green and
pleasant land'. It may be remembered by students of our
literature that the district peculiarly delighted the two greatest artists in scenery in our history, Wordsworth and Cole-
ridge, whose Somerset cottage home at Nether Stowey is
held by the National Trust. And these 'Lake poets', pre-
judiced in favour of the north-west, exulted also in the
south-west. They felt the surprises of the scenery as well as
its static charms. If you enter the midst of Somerset from the
north, say from Bristol, you regard the Mendip range as an
easy green slope, and indeed the hills are low and tame
even in comparison with other hills in Somerset, with the
Quantocks and Exmoor. But when you pass the crown
they break into splendour and appear to grow in height like
a wave preparing to break. The land wave may have
pushed forward in a southerly direction till checked by
shallower ground when the crest advanced more quickly
than the base. This phenomenon belongs to the greater part
of the ridge; but the Cheddar Gorge is a thing to itself, outside the range of comparison. It is rugged, spectacular, even

Plate 21. The Somerset Plain, near Chillington

gorgeous, a marvellous example of a fact repeatedly illustrated in Britain that size is not essential to grandeur. You
cannot, of course, compare the Cheddar Gorge with the
American canyons, but it inspires wonder and admiration
in a like degree. Nor are the famous caves comparable with
those of Western Australia. Both are hollowed by water
and decorated with fantastic patterns on floor and roof and
wall by the drip of diluted lime built up in stalagmites and
hung down in stalactites like the great wooden pendants of
decorated Gothic. It is the strangeness not the scope that
matters. These caves are one representation of a quality in
the stone of which much of the Mendips, of Ham Hill
even, and of hills round Bath and at Ancaster are composed. It is a lovely stone for the builder, in most of its
forms. The harder Bath stone and the softer Ancaster are
tough enough, but worked without undue difficulty; and
whether outside a building or, in the softer stones, within it,
they show a creamy whiteness so evasive that it suggests
most of the colours of which whiteness is composed. How
should not houses and churches of supreme charm be
raised where such stone offers itself?

In general, it is wisest for those who would maintain the
character of a scene to use the native stone or traditional
substitute; but the granite, most properly used in Cornwall,
is denied the charm of the limestones. It is magnificent, but
it is not peace. The mason dare not face the toil of subduing
it to his own imagination, his own art; and so when worked
into dwellings it keeps some of the starkness that has en-
abled it to fight the pounding sea itself. The granite house
has something of the cliff in it. We must admire the simple

strength of Cornish houses and their truth to the note of their foundations; but for 'strength and beauty met to-gether', we must journey further east and north-east, where the rock is less igneous and less primeval. The greatest of all examples is, perhaps, Bradford-on-Avon.

Somerset owns many rocks, including old red sandstone; but there is no stone here, or perhaps anywhere, which is carved by time and eruptions into lovelier forms than the mountain limestone that makes the foundation and the naked walls of the Cheddar Gorge. The theme or thesis of this book is that the beauty of England is essentially the work of the inhabitants. They have so fashioned their homes and grouped homes, which are villages, their home farms, home parks, home woods and even lakes; their gar-dens and hedges and lanes and paths, that the surface mat-ters supremely. Doubtless every lover of scenery must be in some manner a geologist, and the fascination of geology, always great, is greatest perhaps to the lover of scenery. The botanist knows that the optimum of each plant depends more on lime or its absence than on almost any other in-fluence. The sea and volcanoes were doubtless the first makers of our landscape; but they may be forgotten without great loss, in the home counties—if the phrase may be used outside its technical meaning. The most spectacular excep-tion in the southern part of England is this Cheddar Gorge through the Mendips. The stone goes deep and has been broken by powerful forces. It is made almost wholly of the relics of animal life deposited over the aeons. It has been hardened by pressure, but has remained soft enough to take forms graceful, grand and fantastic. Beauty belongs to it as surely as the leaf to the tree, and the best picture of all in the island is this Cheddar Gorge, so wild and splendid a corridor between scenes as homely as rooms in a house. This crag limestone has other qualities. It forms a number of the loveliest surprises within the island, in the north as in the south, in Derbyshire and Yorkshire, not less than in Somerset.

A slight addition of carbon in the strata may inflict on the scenery a spectacle as grim as the other is beautiful, and there are coal mines near the Mendip Hills; but it remains that carboniferous limestone is as precious in the landscape as Parian marble to a sculptor.

CHAPTER IX

Towards Wales

England is England and nothing else till you approach the Severn and the Wye. Thereabouts Wales is felt at every other turn. The rivers come from the great hills of Wales to tell their tale. Both Severn and Wye rise in the loveliest of them, in Plynlimmon. The Severn takes the more northerly route, and, where it encircles the town and fortress of Shrewsbury, you become aware that it is 'as a moat defensive of a house', defensive against old and else forgotten enemies of England. Hereford is littered with the remnants of both stone and earth fortresses raised against turbulent invaders from the west, some of them surviving from days before accurate history began. Offa's Dyke is not so old as Grimm's Dyke (dug, probably, by a Belgic tribe before the Roman invasion) which makes a nullah well lined with trees and bushes across 'happy, homely Hertfordshire'. King Offa, who probably made the dyke—not continuously but where defence was most urgently needed —flourished in the eighth century after Christ, and from that date upwards the boundaries of England and Wales, save in the extreme south, have been fixed. Worcester is the Roman stronghold of Vigorn; and among the works of nature, not of man, the ten round hills of Malvern that have held their heads up because of the undefeatable gneiss of which they are compounded, suggest to the mind of both

III

Plate 22. Bredon Hill, from the River Avon

geologist and tripper that they are a second line of defence to more westerly hills.

Gloucestershire, which includes the best of the Cotswolds, was always less suggestive of Wales, even when it included Monmouth, for the bit of Wales that is nearest to it is for the most part a plain; and just there, and there only, where the Severn and the Wye come close to one another, it may be said that Wales smacks of England. The plain of Gwint is debatable, and Monmouth has long hovered between two nationalities. Even in its more Cymric part the western side of Gloucestershire remains most English. The Forest of Dean more nearly suggests the New Forest or even Epping than the hill forests of Clun or Radnor. The famous speech-house, known at least as well as any other spot to inhabitants of the west, has a certain savour of Lyndhurst, as Copt Oak, in Charnwood Forest, has not. The road from the Parliament of the forest's management is flanked by open wood that is of the very texture of southern England, so pleasant is the admixture of tree and undergrowth, so various the sorts of tree. Both forests grew timber for the navy, but the bigger timber probably was in Dean. Its great trees are no more, and the art of forestry has been grossly neglected in its regard; but you get a taste of its innate quality, even in oak trees; and some of the hollies are immense beyond the imagination of the east. The glory of the Forest of Dean, which undulates more scenically and more sharply than Charnwood, is such that other less lovely things are subdued to its charm. You do not think of the coal-mines till you are among them. The great stone quarries which cut the landscape like a giant wall on the

Malverns and in Charnwood are more conspicuous, are to some eyes (though certainly not to all) more offensive to the spirit of the place than the coal-mines of the Forest of Dean. Compare, say, Coalville in Leicestershire with Coleford in Gloucester. The carboniferous limestone that creates the highest beauties in our scenery, here refuses to be made ugly. There are some black spots, some depressing mining villages; but in general the fairness of the surface prevails, the complexion is not affected by the wounds. How many people in motor-cars (from which, of course, smaller things whether ugly or lovely are seldom seen)—how many motorists have driven about the forest and never even sus-pected the near neighbourhood of coal-mines and their surface accompaniments!

A certain brotherhood exists between Gloucester, Here-ford and Worcester. They rejoice in the name of 'The Three Counties', as if they alone were the Graces. They celebrate an agricultural show held in rotation at the three capitals—'the Three Counties Show'—a title as proud as the claim of Leicester, Northampton and Rutland to be called, without further qualification, 'The Shires.' Their rivers and their orchards make a true bond between the three cathedral cities; and the three flat green riverine plains, where the Show is held, have a curious likeness, even to the floods that now and then invade them.

How different in most regards is Shropshire; and it is a germane illustration to contrast the site of Shrewsbury with Hereford or Gloucester. Take its northern edge, say the site of the great flower show. On one side of the river the hill is green, but steep almost as a high cliff, and at the top Shrews-

H

bury School enjoys a dry plateau that makes as fair playing fields and as spacious as are seen on the Thames at Eton. That is outside the sharp circle of the river. Inside the slope is abrupt but not high, and avenues of immensely tall elms rim the concavity of the bend and march upwards at inter-vals. The hillock with the quarry in its midst is as splendid a scenic possession as any town may claim; and many towns own park-like spaces that belong properly to the category of rural landscape. Jesmond Dene, for example, on the edge of Newcastle-on-Tyne is a real rival to 'the Quarry' at Shrewsbury.

Trees are said to grow to greater heights in Shropshire than in any other county; and the claim is justified both in the average and in individual examples. They grow, in general, equally well on hill and plain. You look up to wooded hills and down upon orchards and wooded plains. The elms in the Quarry at Shrewsbury are immense on the river's edge; but other trees, not least the oaks, clothe wide spaces of the Wrekin, of Wenlock Edge, and the Clee hills and Caradoc.

The Wrekin standing very abrupt above the Severn towards the north of Shrewsbury town possesses an individ-uality that has scarcely a parallel in hillier districts. It is a lonely hill, belonging to no range or group as the Peak of Derbyshire or Scafell Pike belong. Its shape fills the eye and remains in the memory as clearly as Table Mountain itself. From a distance it may look immense, but it is a friendly hill, green and in parts tree-clad and the crown of it is the view over the valley of the Severn down to Buildwas which is the gateway to another sort of scene. Shropshire and

Hereford are alike in this respect, that they both give the impression of being hilly, Shropshire of being almost mountainous, but the hills belong to the valleys, not the valleys to the hills. It has been very well said (by Mr. Howarth) that many streams look too puny for their valleys, but that the Wye is an exception. It is the palpable creator of its own environment. The Severn is another exception. The Shropshire hills belong to the river. Whichever you climb, the river is the scroll that you wish to read, the scroll on which the story is written. Its wide margins are richly illuminated with meadow and orchard and trees and even towns of which Shrewsbury itself is the crown; but they hardly divert you from the text.

This mastery of the river is most compelling when you look southward and westward from the Wrekin; but like Xenophon's soldiers when they climbed the hill and saw the sea, you cry, 'the Severn, the Severn' when the path from the hollow of Wenlock itself takes you to the top of Wenlock Edge. England contains many 'edges' and the name is accurate and appropriate enough to please the geologist himself. It may be an edge indeed as here and there in the lakes when you may literally stride it, walking with one foot on one side and one on the other. Such edges where surface shale is present may be dangerous to life and limb. Wenlock Edge has no forbidding feature. It is neither very high nor very steep. No contour forbids vegetation; but it is a true edge, representing an upheaval that has been planed down on both sides by various forces that could not destroy the central core. Such edges are wholly other in character and appearance than the escarpments of

the downs or the Cotswolds. It is one of the longest of
edges: there are twenty miles of it for the better part flanking
the Severn. If you ascend from the adorable hollows on the
western side you desire first to look down on the Severn and
its valley; but the views behind you smack as truly of the
nature of Wales as the eastward view of England. The
Long Mynd above others is a mountain in character with a
Cymric character in its dark heights. Shrewsbury town
needed its walls and its castle and its river moat when it was
neighbour to the tribes that lurked in and behind such a
fastness. In such a manner Carlisle was defensive against
the hillmen of the Lakes.

There is more than one hill in Wales named from its
likeness to a sleeping lion; and all along these rich fair
valleys of Shropshire and Hereford and less obviously in
Worcester or Gloucester both scenery and fortifications
suggest an historic hostility between rich people of the
plain and warlike tribes of the hills. Peacock's satiric war-
song of the Welsh chieftain has historic foundations and
contains a present picture:

> *The mountain sheep were sweeter;*
> *But the valley sheep were fatter*
> *We therefore deemed it meter*
> *To carry off the latter.*

The Shropshire sheep with their large frames and solid,
though fine fleeces, are as much a feature of the landscape in
the plain as the dark and active little mountain sheep for
which the hillsides of Wales are famous. To this day the
Shropshire fleeces are especially desired by the local weavers
and spinners in their little factories below the hills.

Hereford is more numerously dotted with antique castles than Shropshire, but there are few pulpits from which the hostile contrast with Wales is better seen than a vantage point or two on Wenlock Edge, when you turn your back on the Severn valley and look westward towards the Long Mynd and Church Stretton. An historic fear of Welsh invaders or rebels is expressed in the capitals of both Shropshire and Cheshire. It has been pointed out that early settlements, the nuclei of towns began under the shadow of the castles; weaker and richer folk sought efficient protection. They often built defences for their own houses but they relied in the last instance on the stronghold of the castle. It has happened that a number of our more beautiful towns, or less ugly towns, are those that were first built up for the sake of the castle, which was their one hope of safety. The castles themselves were raised where the nature of the country, especially hill and river, gave defensive help. It was so at Ludlow, which offers, from the granite hill over the river, as satisfying an urban view as any in the island. Even Chepstow is hardly grander. It was so at Chester and at Shrewsbury. Most of the scores of fortresses which the fearful Saxons and Romans thrust forward into Wales have an architecture infinitely enhanced by their site; Car/narvon, Harlech and Manorbier are characteristic examples. Everyone who has driven along a road knows how steep the opposite hill looks when you descend a slope towards it. That sort of exaggeration impresses those who look towards the Welsh hills from the north side of the valley of the Dee, a beautiful river, beautifully bridged; and the city of Chester has advanced from one sort of beauty to another. What is

Plate 23. Looking towards Wales from Longmynd,
above Church Stretton

Tudor and what was Roman consent to a mutual relation
that is wholly pleasing, in spite of unlovely additions of
later centuries. Cheshire is not regarded as one of the most
lovely of counties. It has many flat green plains that are a
dairyman's paradise, but hardly a scenic wonder; yet it
possesses, even close to the edge of some of the great towns,
a rural feature almost peculiar to itself. Some of the
Cheshire meres are at least as pleasing as the Norfolk
Broads, and as well fitted to be natural sanctuaries. The
harvest of observation reaped in them by such famous
observers as Mr. Coward, who is a standard authority on
birds, is not excelled by the students of Hickling Broad,
which is said to have made a naturalist of every man and
woman in the neighbourhood. They are subdued to the
country they live in. Marbury Mere is one good example.
Though almost at its edge the elms wither and tilt as the
salt is drawn from the soil beneath them, though the great
country house, with its hundred bedrooms and hardly less
roomy stables, is long past its heyday, the mere keeps the
character of a sort of lake that is hardly found in other parts
of the island. Old Tabley Mere, which inspired much of
the sonorous verse of Lord de Tabley, that much under-
rated poet, is true to the same type, though multitudes of
stag-headed oaks suggest the approach of its doom. That
most scenic of all birds, the wild swan (of three species) is
peculiarly attracted to the meres. For the rest, in spite of
several glorious views of distant Welsh hills, Cheshire is not
influenced by Welsh scenery as are Shropshire and Hereford, which are invincibly 'border'.

Hereford has a hundred castles, but only one or two of

them became the nucleus of considerable towns. The absence of industrial towns is an addition, though of a negative sort, to the claims of Hereford to be the most uniformly
beautiful county in England. It is without excess in any
feature; and possesses no spot that excels the rest unless it be
Symonds Yat where the Wye has cut the hard hillstone into
the likeness of a cliff. Hazlitt was called an epicure by
Stevenson because he demanded for his full aesthetic satisfaction a bend in the road. He was a born walker. So the
born boatman demands a bend in the river, and the Wye
thereabouts is as sinuous as a snake, not like 'the Huntingdon Ouse', because it cannot make up its mind which is the
easiest passage through the even valley, but because it must
circumvent the hard core of obstinate hills.

A votary of other counties might perhaps say of Hereford
that in regard to hills (though certainly not in regard to
rivers or cultural surface) it owes the crown of its glorious
views to its neighbours. This is true. On one side the blue
walls of the Hay Bluff and the so-called Black Mountains,
on the other the salience of the Clee hills of Shropshire are
the features that most emphatically impress the eye when
you seek the two finest prospects in Hereford. So also, if you
wish to see Snowdonia trapped out in its full majesty you
will cross the Menai Straits into the flatness of Anglesey and
look eastwards over Carnarvon. You mount a hill to see
what is below it. You must retire, as an artist retires from a
picture, to admire the hill itself. There is no Wrekin in
Hereford, no salient edge, no commanding ridge; but the
foreground of its most splendid views is singularly rich,
partly from the green meadows on which the white-faced

Herefords fatten, but chiefly from the continual uprising of hills clothed with trees.

Below Hereford, is a hill as well and carefully rounded as the Malverns, though again tall trees of many species in some degree hide its conformation. The singularly lovely village of Credenhill mounts the slope to the point where the wood begins. The village in its setting may be compared with Selborne. A very deeply trenched Roman camp, probably successor to a British, crowns the top but invisibly, for it is overgrown with trees including some old yews used as a gymnastic playing ground by the badgers that have their earths in the Roman vallum. There are perhaps few places in England which better illustrate what may be called the continuity of the English landscape. The changes have been great, have been crucial, but the signs of the past are legible as the geology is legible on the very surface. The gates of houses in the village are topped with worked stone of a visibly different substance from the rest of the structure. Some of the old walls and a part of the beautiful, humble old church are of the same grey stone. These stones are relics of the older Roman town that was built on the broad green meadow below the hill. If your walk should take you into the country round about, you will find curious hollows in wood and field, and you are driven to the inference that these were the quarries from which the Romans quarried the stone for their township.

The whole conformation at the top of the hill is altered by the digging of the ditches and ramparts for the great camp which is about a mile and a quarter in circumference. More than this, the scooped Roman road which leads to it

becomes apparent to all eyes before you reach the woodland
that has embraced hill and camp. The trees themselves tell
stories. About the road is an avenue of oaks probably
seven or eight hundred years of age, eloquent in their girth
and in their decay of the centuries they have seen. The other
trees which are of many sorts, including Scotch fir, ash,
maple, wych-elm, yew, are much younger. A forester
could make a fair guess at the age of the veterans. None was
there in the days of Elizabeth; and it is no surprise to find an
old print in a cottage showing a round hill with a smooth
grassy crown. Where to-day the rabbits nibble off the carpet
of seedling ash, sheep once grazed on sweet grasses and the
shepherd could gaze without interruption on the few relic
ruins of the Roman town and the glorious valley of the Wye
beyond it. The present wood, as happens too often in
English woods, is perhaps lovelier for its neglect. Wood-
pecker and nuthatch rejoice in rotting trunk and bough.
Many a great tree now quite valueless would have boasted a
taller and straighter trunk, most desirable in the eyes of the
timber merchant, if its superfluous boughs had been
lopped, its misshapen neighbours cut down and the stag-
headed trees felled these many years. The one compensation
for this common loss of national wealth, this absence of
what Theodore Roosevelt called conservation, is that what
has come into being is exceedingly beautiful. A well
forested wood is beautiful too, but with a beauty of another
sort.

A more famous hill to the north of Hereford advertises a
yet older history. It is as famous among geologists as among
tourists. Backbury Hill, often but wrongly called Black-

bury, proclaims its strange birth to all who enter the wood
at its summit; and at one place on the ascent even to the
rapid traveller by car. The walls and shafts of granite thrust
up through other strata suggest some sudden and gigantic
explosion when the hard rocks were a molten fluid.
Another view that some hold to be one of the very finest in
England meets the eyes of those who play golf or stop their
car on the road at the edge of the links not far from the
western edge of Hereford itself. A wide area of the low
green hills of the county are the foreground and away behind them setting the flourish on the prospect are the Clee
hills, grouped like a bouquet of flowers against the northern sky. The place has not the reputation of the scores of
'beacons' scattered about England. The famous Brecon
Beacon not far away to the westward has a wider, a more
wonderful sweep, but for satisfying wealth of colour,
especially shades of green and blue, for continuity of tree-
scape, wood-scape, field-scape, the northern and western
view from this place has few peers, perhaps no superiors.
There is a gap in the hedge that is an open door to the
very sanctum of west country splendour.

In few other districts do you pass so quietly and so
quickly from the little scene to the big. You may walk from
the west bank of the Wye and watch the rise of the salmon
without other thought than the river itself, its pools and its
reaches. You need travel no further than across a green
meadow and up a gentle lane to find yourself by a farmhouse where spread before you lies a great part of Herefordshire in the foreground and further back the hills or
mountains of Shropshire, of Radnor and of Brecknock.

Now and again, though not often, the river confesses its Welsh and mountainous source. As you watch it, the level rises with startling vehemence. On its current come floating down first the debris caught on the low boughs of the willows, then the eggs and, it may be, the complete nests of moor-hens; and if the downpour in the Welsh hills has been tremendous, the victims may include farm stock. The river is capable of rising twelve feet within two hours. Such is the passion of a Welsh origin.

A view as characteristic as any is spread before you as soon as you escape from the western suburbs of Hereford. Adam's Hill may or may not have any association with the Garden of Eden, but the view from it is singularly eloquent of the higher virtues of the west country. You look across the Wye, very green and well treed; and both in the valley and on its slopes and undulations the land is rich. The ruddy soil is peculiarly favourable to the apple, and orchard after orchard is gay in flower-time and fruit-time with Fox's Whelp and Blackstone and Bulmer's Norman and Med-aille d'Or and scores of others of the bittersweet apples out of which cider is made and has been made for the last eight hundred years and more. As you swing round and look through the trees over Hereford direct on to very flat plains about the river, like Worcester and like Gloucester, you see the round hills of Malvern, and find once again that the crown of the Herefordshire view is the hill of another shire.

Most of the rivers of the marshes change as they enter England. The Severn, which cuts out a steep narrow valley near the border, is famous for the rich orchards about it. Its mountainous character has wholly departed. No other area in England—not even the silt land of south Lincolnshire or the orchards beside the Avon at Evesham—is more essen/ tially fertile than the valley of the Teme above Tenbury. The fruit orchards, the hop fields, the general farm, the lush meadows come into close touch and all flourish. The steep ridge towards the north and west gives shelter; the soil has all the virtues and the river gives the moisture and the drainage. All along those reaches you are aware of the intensive productiveness. Some share in the fertility of the district must be allowed to the upland gardens and farms about the timbered houses dotted thickly, though the closest neighbours are invisible to one another among the trees and sudden hollows all about the Shropshire and Worcestershire border.

The valley of the Teme is the most palpably fertile, but the Wye excels, in all eyes except the farmer's, in scenic virtue. It possesses every quality. As the salmon know, it flows fast but has deep pools. It is patently deflected by firm ridges pleasantly covered with trees. Sometimes little spin/ neys come down to the banks on either side, interrupting the flat green meadows. It is rarely but most beautifully bridged. Wye, like Teme, always seems to wish to keep close to the county of its origin. It is a border stream making a defensive line and at a score of convenient places where high land bounds the stream, castles have been built at many dates. William the Conqueror, who made the cities of Chester, Shrewsbury and Worcester into the headquar/ ters of his defensive system, succeeded to the work of the Romans in the first century and of King Offa (whose dyke

Plate 24. A cherry orchard at Ledbury,
Herefordshire

extended from the Dee to the estuary of the Wye) in the
eighth century. The power of Llewellyn and Glendower
maintained the need of defence to the fifteenth century. No
castles are more spectacular than those on the Wye. Good-
rich and Chepstow perhaps come first; but in the association of man-made and nature-made beauties, Chepstow is
perhaps supreme. Here indeed 'a splendour falls on castle
walls'.

River and bridge and trees and the very names of the old
places are eloquent of a high romance. All that is fair in all
rivers comes into epitome below Tintern, which is a name
to conjure with. Not even Caerleon upon Usk excels it.

CHAPTER X

The South of Wales

Of the many, yet surprisingly few doors into mid Wales—for bridges over Wye and Severn are not very numerous—none presents the new character of the scene more persuasively than the junction of Hereford with Radnor and Brecon by the Hay Bluff. The angle of that masterful hill suggests the cliff of a sea. It stays on the mind like a Matterhorn. It impresses the eye from a distance, especially from the high ground just out of Hereford city on the west side. You point and say: 'There are the Black Mountains,' almost as if they were a place of hidden mystery, into whose doors a pied piper might vanish. That sense remains, though the real fear of them belongs to the list of old unhappy far-off things.

Distance may lend grimness as well as enchantment, and a certain grimness touches the Black Mountains almost up to the moment you enter their pale. The most English and eastern of the five chief valleys that belong to this part of the range, the Olchon Valley, is curiously remote. An isolated farm-house here and there has a medieval air that the look of the inmates does not altogether dissipate. The little stream flowing between meadows, where the wild daffodils are very much at home (asserting their claim to be native against botanical doubters) disappears from time to time under the flanking bushes. It is not bridged, even where the road crosses it. Instead concrete has been set on the floor of it, with a passage or two below it, which accommodates a good part of the water while the rest flows over the top of the concrete. It is a change from the magnificent old bridges over the Herefordshire Wye, which are being pre-served, even when widening is necessary, by the County Council, who in this regard at any rate give a model for all other counties to imitate.

Beyond the river and parallel with it, the hills justify their name of blackness, even at so close a range, even when their tops are white with snow, as may happen in spring itself. Yet they are the friendliest hills when you find your-self amongst them, though queerly deceptive in contour and pattern. The very elect may lose his sense of direction. The Hay Bluff, where it is circumvented by the Wye, may be likened to the handle of a fan that is three parts closed, and you may easily mistake, if new to the district, which valley, which road you are pursuing, whether you are heading to points that belong to Hereford or Abergavenny.

The chief of the valleys is 'The Golden Valley', and its name will indicate how completely the sentiment of the place has changed for those who have the freedom of it. Some of the minor roads have every charm that belongs to an unhedged way. English roads, since enclosure began, are almost all hedged. The hedges are part of the proper beauty of 'the humanised scene', but some visitors complain that they are apt to conceal the landscape unduly. It is some-times so, but there is a virtue in what 'half reveals and half conceals' that is missed by patent completeness. What an artistic pleasure to stop a car at a gap or low place in a hedge and to behold a view framed like a picture, composed like a picture, individual as a picture and endowed with the power of a great picture to engrave itself on the mind's eye.

The unhedged road is a pleasant change nevertheless—at any rate for those who can endure the waste of time that is involved in opening rickety gates. Half-wild Welsh ponies belonging to a race unequalled in the island, show their fire and their paces as they cross your way! The plover rise almost under your wheels and circle above the car. You drive and yet lay hands on some of the booty of the walker; but here, as in all hills, the man on his feet sees things that other sorts of travellers miss.

One of the finest views of the Black Mountains is from their southern extremity; the famous Sugar Loaf Hill of Monmouth. It stands high and isolated over the town of Abergavenny and the valley of the Usk. You may soon walk up its two thousand feet, but the rough paths and rough country towards its base are as deceptive as any roads about the Golden Valley. From the peak you can see almost every sort of hill, the long, dark range of the rest of the Black Mountains, the twin peaks of the Beacons and, to the east, Skirrid Fawr, a hill of legend and myth to which even Monmouth has no parallel. Thereabouts the scenery that is characteristic of Wales melts into a soft, a varied fertility that becomes pure England in the valley of the lower Wye and the Severn.

The mountains and valleys that lead towards Aber-gavenny are utterly unlike the high hills such as Clyro Hill on the northern side of the Wye and in Radnor. These are barer and more easily defined, and incredibly empty of

population. There are not so many as 20,000 folk within the county. You travel for miles and see not a single house, and some of the homesteads that you discover are on the edge of wide stretches of heather, or of scrub and marsh that are as wild in nature as any places within Britain. There is one great highland marsh, of Rhos-Goch, that is the water-shed of streams flowing in opposite directions, which feels, and indeed looks, almost primeval. Part of it is overgrown with low scrub, chiefly of birch, and the passage through its hummocky moisture is an adventure made well worth-while by the songs of warblers. The greater part is a genuine marsh, and the wildness of it is enhanced by the number of seagulls, of the black-headed species which cry overhead in a plausible likeness to a pack of hounds in full tongue. It is the nursery of these alleged sea-birds, and of good quantity of duck as well. The wildest of all bird notes is a common sound. Nesting curlew haunt its edges and wail over the heads of any disturber of their peace. The immense stretch of unpeopled areas in this region of Wales has left the free-dom to numbers of wild birds and some half-cultivated birds. You may see a merlin rise from the turf butts—many of them singularly solid—built for the destruction of the grouse which flourish on the moors. There was a buzzard's nest, built in a larch representing the relic of a vain attempt at afforestation, which was left undisturbed for so long that the bird finally heaped up a sort of cornucopia—as the shape suggested—not less than seven feet in depth. With your feet on the bough holding the first nest you were still unable to look into the newest nursery.

The whole neighbourhood suggests some of the Scottish

I

Plate 25. Llanthony Abbey, in one of the Black Mountain valleys

moors, but remains wholly individual. It is not a far cry to the Elan Valley, which may be taken as a scenic type of the vast water reservoirs made necessary by the huge towns. Birmingham is the final cause of the transformation of the Elan Valley, as the Lancashire towns of Lake Vyrnwy.

It is allowable for those who knew the undisturbed little stream at the foot of the valley, who worshipped in the church or dwelt in the hamlet, to lament the desecration of their country. Yet the scene is beautiful, is even magnifi-cently beautiful after its kind. The three great dams, as broadly based almost as the Pyramids themselves, have their own architectural grandeur, and the spacious roads that lead to them and over them give views that have been created by the transformation. Behind the highest dam the stream that has become an immense lake has gained in glory what it lost in domesticity. Even the trout that inhabited it have grown bigger with the waters and more numerous. The hills enclosing most of the large northern reservoirs have been afforested by the municipalities which have made the lakes, and one is apt to associate pine-clad slopes with such reservoirs, in England as in South Africa.

The Elan waters excelling in area rather than in depth, are banked by lower heathery hills of an easier acclivity, and for the most part only the floor of the scene has been changed. It is all very beautiful, of that there can be no question. On the ruins of antique beauty a new beauty is raised, and yet it is not altogether new, for the old coloured hills encircle it and subdue even the concrete dams to their influence.

Britain is full of 'forests', but of them all Radnor Forest

best deserves the name when we have realised that the word does not imply the presence of trees. Trees there are on the lower parts of Radnor, and the ring-ousel nests at their edge in surprising numbers; but the greater stretches are un-peopled wastes with much heather. Here if anywhere, you may feel remote. Even that almost extinct bird, certain sign of a wild country, the kite, has nested thereabouts, and the curlew nests in good numbers there as at the edge of the marsh of Rhos-Goch. Unlike the lakes or the Yorkshire moors, it is not neighbour to any great town or succession of towns and is no one's playground, unless the naturalist's or the sportsman's. Even the tripper from a distance is a rare bird. In parts of eastern England, especially in Hunting-don, the population was falling both steadily and rapidly for the fifty years or so that preceded the end of the great war. In this part of Britain on both sides of the border—almost as notably in Hereford as in Radnor—the popula-tion has been falling for a hundred years at least, at a slow, steady rate; the compensation is a landscape that has suf-fered less from the common outrages—from ill-coloured, bungaloid growths, from ribbon development, from ad-vertisements of a raucous character, from roads that pro-claim their contempt of contour or environment, from litter, from barbed wire—than any other area of equal size within England or Wales. If you lose your way you will scarcely find anyone to set you right. Radnor cuts into the middle of Wales, and though it belongs technically to South Wales (which is a third larger than North Wales) it is scenically a country to itself. Wales is narrow at the waist. The distance from Clun Forest (at the juncture of Shropshire, Hereford,

Radnor and Montgomery) to the sea at Aberystwyth is less than fifty miles. It is a neglected, almost a despised district, but you will hardly see its like again wherever you may travel, to the north or the south, to Snowdonia or the Brecon Beacons, but it belongs to the south.

One guide-book to South Wales is entitled *Brecon and South Wales*, with Brecon in large capitals; and no journey —by train, by car, or on foot, passes through such hills and valleys, so Welsh in character as the way between Aver-gavenny, a border town, and Merthyr Tydvil. The rail is one of the highest in the kingdom, for railways cling to valleys where they can, and it is the one objection to rail-ways as a vantage point for the observer as analyst of the landscape—that they show us no hills. As soon as a rise is threatened comes the cutting, a most effective sort of blinker, or the tunnel. Yet even here the walker may look down on the railway many hundreds of feet below him. The Beacons of Brecknockshire or Brecon are a walker's paradise, scarcely surpassed by any mountain scenery in North Wales. His chief danger or obstruction comes from marshes that are as native to the Welsh hills as to Dartmoor or an Irish plain.

South Wales in general, in spite of its Cader Idris, its Plynlimmon and the beacons, is a gentler place than North Wales. Geographers call it a flat plateau, sloping to sea-side levels. At one time such gentleness extended to the inhabi-tants. Agricola found the Silures amenable and the Ordo-vici terrible. The great camp, that still bears its unqualified name of Chester, was the base for other disciplinary camps that penetrated the country even to the edge of Carnarvon

Castle. The great plain of Cheshire, now the centre of the busiest dairying industry in the country, suitable to its flat green fields, was always in danger from the men of the hills. The plain of Gloucester and Monmouth extends across the valleys of the Wye and Severn and through Monmouth up to the neighbourhood of the Usk, creating some sort of sympathy between the dwellers on either side of the boundaries. There is perhaps a certain parallelism to the scenic nature of Cheshire and Flint; but the ground within that little county rises steeply to the fastnesses where once the warriors dwelt and threatened. Yet within South Wales is one great storm centre, both human and geological. No other formation within the island bears any near likeness to 'The Valleys', as they are often called without qualification, of Monmouth and Glamorgan, where have been delved the most famous coal-mines of the world. Much of the comely grandeur of the hills has been destroyed within the last hundred and fifty years by the development of both iron and coal; but there is a sharp geological distinction which is expressed in the boundaries of the purely scenic desecration. The great mining towns such as Aberdare, or Mountain Ash or Merthyr, begin where the old red sandstone ridge of Brecon runs almost parallel with the carboniferous limestone ridge to the south. The depression between them has been used as rabbits use a convenient bank for tunnelling their holes.

The development of the mineral wealth was of course inevitable, was a thing to be welcomed; but the process began when the mad pursuit of what was held to be national prosperity clean blinded our population to the obligations of beauty and health. The builders, even of Johannesburg, were more thoughtful than the builders of Glamorganshire's mining towns and villages. The compensation is that there is an ever quicker escape to the glories of Brecknock than the lakes offer to the crowded populations of industrial Lancashire, or the Pennines to Yorkshire industrialists.

The Beacons are glorious; and the rivers, which include the Usk and the Towy, have lovely cradles, though the marshes are deep and even dangerous. The sources of the rivers are close together as the crow flies. A succession of smaller streams have hustled their way in a tolerably direct line towards the sea, and have chiselled out abrupt valleys, each very like its neighbour, on a map, but on no other view, unless your aeroplane flies very high and dwarfs the country to a Mosaic. Both wild and cultivated beauty are closely juxtaposed to the ugliness associated, alas, with most mines and mining towns and villages. It is difficult to find aesthetic value either in a slag heap or a slate roof. Yet even a slag heap may be the vile body of a fair experiment. At Aberdare and other places valiant efforts have been made to make the desert blossom as the rose; and it was happily discovered that yellow broom, which grows as readily as the Cymric species of gorse in Snowdonia, is a stout reclaimer. It will flourish in shale, and what is more, create conditions for larger and smaller growths of a more fastidious nature. Even chestnut trees will flourish on some of the reclaimed slag heaps or 'tips'. The reclamation of tips is a proper art in the annals of the humanised scene.

One of the troubles to houses as well as to trees, new and

old, is the subsidence of the upper soil following the tunnelling of the mines. The trouble is not of the scale to be seen in Cheshire, in the region of Nantwich, where whole houses are sometimes embraced in chains, underlaid by beams, and bodily lifted from the scoop into which they have begun to fall. You see thereabouts towering trees in a fair scene, turn yellow and tilt and fall, and the character of a scene shift as quickly as if a firm of speculative builders were following their usual and abominable habit of clearing the place of its bigger timber.

The coalmines have no such sudden, general effect as this. Their waste heaps are more in evidence than their crevasses, but the houses crack and tilt imperceptibly and the task of maintenance may be continuous. These sudden valleys, once havens of natural beauty, have no little surface fertility. The prosperity of the mines led to some neglect of the other resources of Glamorgan and Monmouth, but since the trade in export coal diminished and unemployment became a constant enemy, the husbandry of the valleys has been revived and is being further extended. Perhaps nothing so good of its kind is to be found within Britain as the halfcommunal farms that begin to flourish about the places where unemployment lies heaviest on the land.

The Usk and all these parallel streams belong wholly to Monmouth and to Wales and are of one nature from start to finish. Wales passes on her two greatest rivers to England. The Wye and the Severn are both cradled on Plynlimmon at no great distance from one another. It is a mightily romantic mountain, and dismisses these two rivers towards

the east, but thereabouts are other lesser streams which make
a short journey, though the route is often crooked, towards
the western sea. The bridge over one of them, the Rheidol,
is the centre of a reach of scenery that is unsurpassed. Everyone knows of the Devil's Bridge, which has a rich solidity
of its own and is an admirable focus, and few streams so
persuasively elucidate the methods by which a valley is
carved out. But the particular inspiration of the scene is the
accompaniment of wooded heights from which you can
look down upon the crooked course of the rivers or up their
narrow ravines. Free and rapid growth is native to the
region. There is a spacious, deserted garden thereabouts,
famous in poetry, where rhododendrons grow to immense,
almost Asiatic, size as if this little Welsh stream were the
Brahmaputra, and even vertical rocks are clothed with self-
sown seedlings. The wild yellow poppy of Wales flourishes
near by.

It is a due acknowledgment of the value of the Welsh
rivers to the scene that the names of a succession of towns
announce the reason of their existence: Aberystwyth, Aberdovey, Barmouth. It must not be discussed which is the
most lovely. It is an old tale that two Britons meeting
abroad argued fiercely about the nature of the loveliest walk
in Britain. One said: 'From Barmouth to Dolgelly.' The
other: 'From Dolgelly to Barmouth.' A third disputant
might well have put in a claim for any of several walks
round about the Devil's Bridge in the hinterland of Aberystwyth. That popular seaside resort, which is also the
site of part of the University, has no supreme attractions,
though the stone circle within its circumference is quaint

and interesting; but the hills behind it, which spill the rivers into the narrow plain are of a rare and rich beauty. It is one of the sins against the light, though not very offensive to the eye, that the decanting of mechanical rubbish into the waters has quite driven the Atlantic salmon from congenial breeding beds.

This is a coastal excursion towards North Wales. To the south is 'Little England Beyond Wales', Pembrokeshire, where Flemings were settled to keep the Welsh in order and the English language prevails over the Welsh. Milford, one of the finest and safest harbours in the world, penetrates far back into that wonderful promontory. The big harbour contains little harbours, such as Dale; there are safe anchorages all the way. The mouth is well guarded and narrow enough. The general scene is of rare beauty as where the trees dip their feet in the water by the estuary of Sandy Hook. In due season the waters teem with fish, with mackerel, whitingpollock, gurnet and a score besides. Yet this supreme harbour has been treated as almost useless, as an inlet of small account. The nation has disregarded it. Once, at its point of deepest penetration, there were active docks, at Pembroke, but they too, were at last closed. Docks there are at Milford, and there are signs of revival, but was ever a humbler town found on so glorious a site! It is a scarcely credible fact that the Great Western Railway, desiring a harbour (for Irish traffic) thought it better to blast out a hillside and throw out a breakwater, at immense expense, just across the way, when so ideal a harbour lay to their hand; but the main railway always shirked Milford. Yet no harbour—not Liverpool, Bristol, Falmouth, Ply mouth, Portsmouth, or Southampton Water, or Dover, can endure comparison with the Cinderella that Milford has always been. The very latest book dealing with the scenery of our island dismisses the harbour in a brief reference to the 'inlet'. Could the figure of speech which grammarians call meiosis or belittlement further go? In general the seaside places looking westward do not owe so apparent a debt to the rivers as the more southerly towns. The estuary of the Dovey is beloved of fishermen (and of sewin), but Aberdovey owes its attractions to other causes—to its dunes and reeds and the wellclad hills of the hinterland. They nurse lovely gardens and sheep farms, whose one enemy is the encroaching bracken. Aberystwyth gives no air of being a seaside town. It leans on its hills.

Of a very different sort is the inherent virtue of Swansea and Newport, on the Towy and the Usk ; or indeed, of Cardiff. Perhaps Cardiff, of all towns in the island, is the most superior to its general reputation among those who do not know it. It is open and spacious, well fitted for a great University. Though much smaller, Towy and Usk may be called rivals of Wye and Severn. Swansea itself is not a Bristol, and owes more to its sea than its river. Has any big place by the sea—even Llandudno with its proud and tremendous Orme's Head—so original a seaside 'scape as the Mumbles? Or is there any change so quick and complete as meets those who descend from the tinplate works of Llanelly just to the north, through the industries of Swansea and continue their way to the mouth of the river and the Gower Peninsula? The sunsets thereabouts are as famous as the sunsets of the eastern Fens, where the lowland mist plays the part of the sea and the willows of the rocks. The Mumbles are deservedly famous. They offer all the charms of the western coast: high cliffs of curious pattern, pleasant coves and bays, and spacious views. The peninsula guards Carmarthen Bay on the south as Tenby and Caldy Island on the north. One of the curiosities is a raised beach such as is found, though at a greater height and more salient form on the Isle of Jura, and such as provide the foundation of Spittals in Northumberland. The hills that decant their mineral wealth at Swansea and Cardiff are glorious; yet if a generalisation be allowed—and within Britain any scenic generalisation is apt to be false—South Wales is glorious for its valleys and North Wales for its mountains. You must travel, preferably by road, from Carmarthen to Abergavenny and Monmouth to know what a long valley may be in the Welsh sense. Follow the Towy and make acquaintance with the best of Wales. It may not carry the very finest gems—unlike the Wye it has no Chepstow, whose bridge, with the yellow wall-flowers perennial in the stones, the seductive surprises of the river bends, and the romance of its association with Caerleon well below it, or Tintern above it. The valley of the Usk is certainly more splendid, more salient, but the Towy has a character scarcely found further east. Its own valley may conceal the river that made it. You are often conscious, chiefly of the scoop itself and the long declivity arrased with green trees. South Wales is dimpled with miniature valleys of this sort, miniature copies of the carvings of the more famous rivers. Often you have some ado to come near the stream, half buried in vegetation. A small and lovely example is a tiny stream that flows through a narrow valley into the small, highly-walled harbour of Solva in Pembrokeshire. It is a surprise when near the bottom of the valley, the stream appears in the open, flowing over a water-wheel. It is more of a surprise to find a factory in being, if a local craft may be so called, where the fleeces of local sheep are spun and woven into stuffs. Another of no greater size flows through the city of St. David's, between the Cathedral and the gorgeous ruin of the Bishop's Palace. The Cathedral itself is modestly built within a narrow valley and is scarcely visible from the inland side till you come almost on the top of it. The stream partakes of the general modesty. It has a trick of disappearing quite, yet as you see it vanish among stones (or lower down among stunted trees and lush water plants) you find it an apt illustration of the best river line in literature:

Fluminaque antiquos subterlabentia muros.

Its banks everywhere outside the city (which is itself a hamlet) are wild and uncultivated, beloved of many flowers and many birds. It writhes its humble way to the sea to form a delectable 'porth' or estuary that will give harbourage to one or two, or perhaps even three, fishing boats or launches.

The lanes are often rather like the rivers. They lead for the most part to some isolated holding or house, and those who walk down them are invisible to the rest of the world as the spotted trout in the stream. The tall and solid banks that enclose the lanes are rock gardens, most artistically planted with dwarf flowers, with sheep's bit, foxglove and pennywort, set between gorse and honeysuckle and fern. What human labour went to their making and how soon nature claimed them!

If any river has an English likeness it is the Teifi, which forms the boundary between Pembroke and Cardigan, the gentlest but not the least fair of Welsh counties.

South Wales maintains its contrast with North Wales right up to the boundary.

CHAPTER XI

The Wall of the Pennines

Wales is much more sharply divided from England than is Scotland though it has a much longer boundary. Just below the line along which England joins Scotland the island is very narrow, at the narrowest seventy-three miles, and there are points towards the northern end of the Pennines where you feel between two seas almost as definitely as when you stand on the grim, barren peak of Brown Willy, in the midst of the slender promontory that is Cornwall. The mouth of the Tyne and the Solway Firth are neighbours. The narrowness rather than the contour has been the reason for one old line of division. As you come up towards the frontier you think less of the rising Cheviots (which, like the white sheep that take their name, are half English) than of Hadrian's Wall, that marvel of Roman engineering and organisation. It was the greatest but not the first artificial division in these parts. Hadrian built it, north of Agricola's military road and his vallum, at an incredible speed for so mighty a work. It was twenty feet high and eight broad with successive forts capable of holding his cohorts. It stretched from Bowness on Solway, just west of the green and gorgeous railway bridge across the Solway, through Carlisle to the coal-mine that is still called Wall's End. Most of it, being made of stone and not of earth, has disappeared owing to the iconoclasm of General

142

Wade and other road makers, but what remains is singu⁄
larly impressive. The tracks of the wheels left in the solid
stone paving of the archways impress you with the reality of
its history, and the placing of the forts often on the crest of
the rise, give them a scenic quality like the stones of Stone⁄
henge. You meet every sort of scenery along its course. The
valley by Carlisle is green and soft. The first fort of which
considerable ruins remain is on the uplands, giving a view
of the valley on one side, of high hills on the other. When
the wall leaves Cumberland for Northumberland it is soon
among moors still wild and untenanted, and in the Roman
way it disregards either the height of the hill or the depth of
the glen. The fort of Vindolana is in the depths, the fort of
Borcovicus on a cliff of basalt and the best⁄known fort of
all, at Chesters, is about a hundred yards from the Tyne,
and the most easterly is supplanted by the industrial streets
of Newcastle. That vanished fort was once, perhaps, as
lovely as the fort of Silurnum some twenty miles away,
where still the landscape keeps its ancient charm. The river
is bright and flows fast; and the high moors on its western
side shelter the rich and well⁄treed valley. You can scarcely
believe that a river with an upper reach of such natural
quality can so soon tumble into scenic ruin.

Such changes as this are common to the three counties of
Northumberland, Durham and York. You are pitched of a
sudden from the summit of beauty into depths of which the
less said the better. The beauty may belong to town and
city as well as open country. Is any building in Europe
more gloriously placed than Durham Cathedral? Is any
region fuller of gloom, especially in our days, than the

'depressed area' near by, with Jarrow in the forefront? If there is any place where the characters of Scotch and English landscape are sharply juxtaposed it is near the middle of the wall at Whin Sill crags. The wild rocks and the dark waters are themselves more Scotch than English, but from this point and that you see, if you look south, a progressively humanised landscape. If you look north, the rough moorland looks unending. The prospect from the stern rock above the Housestead camp appealed especially to that ingenious analyst of scenic qualities, Professor Vaughan Cornish, and he chose his text well. The Pennines, which are usually described by instructional geographers as the backbone of England, would be themselves perhaps Caledonian in character if it were not for the views over lower ground that proclaim the quality of Yorkshire and Lancashire. What is best, and worst, in the English landscape, is the cultivated field and the spreading factory. On parts of the Roman wall you feel that it was designed on purpose to distinguish rival scenes, and it was indeed so placed as to give the widest possible view northwards. It was a succession of watch-towers first and a fortress second. It gave opportunity for the concentration of troops along the Roman road behind it. In English days that road was ballasted like the farm roads round Avebury by the wicked process of breaking up the historic stones. They were the metal nearest to hand.

It is truer of the Pennines than of most country, though it is true of all, that to savour it rightly you must walk, must practise 'the delicate and gentle art of never getting there'; but along the course of such a road as Wade's, the motor-

Plate 26. The Yorkshire Moors in Winter

car gives a landscape scene that is new and wonderful. The railways keep too low in the valleys, the aeroplane flies too high, but the car, taking a bee-line over hill and dale gives to a great ridge or succession of ridges, the familiarity of a mound or a ridge and furrow. Even very familiar scenery can be enhanced by such a view. The passage from the North Downs into the Weald is one good example, but perhaps the Roman road is the best of all, for it takes you almost from sea to sea, and from sea level to a watch-tower of more then two thousand feet.

The triangle of English land between the line of wall and the Tweed has for its eastern boundary the finest reach of the eastern coast, if the Bempton Cliffs of Yorkshire (where the guillemots breed in hundreds) is excepted. Pilgrims to Hexham with its antique and beautifully restored abbey or to the fields of Otterburn and Flodden pass through a fair country of field and moor and fell, separated from the Scottish Lowlands by the Tweed and the Cheviot Hills, which are a paradise for the shepherd. More of those who visit Chesters or Hadrian's Wall would be wise to penetrate this unspoilt and lovely region to the north. It is as often passed by and it as little deserves neglect as Gallo-way over the Solway Firth.

Thirty miles or so south of the steepest fort in the Roman wall is Cross Fell, with a host of pikes round about it. Here is a central fortress that no man built and no man can destroy; to make a more vital similitude, here are the essen-tial vertebrae of England, the focus of the structure near the head. If you started to walk the length of England south-wards along its centre, you would begin at the highest

K

point, and not at one highest point, rather at a cliff that ran at a continuous height for many more miles than you would compass in a day's walk. The Lakes and Cheviots have no fell so high, much less have they so high and broad an area of elevation. From Appleby to Cross Fell is the most necessary of all the walks that must be taken for an under-standing of the beauty of England. If there is any doubt about the aesthetic supremacy of the scene, whether you look over the ridge west or down to Dales east, it is seen that few peaks adorn a salience like the Wrekin or even a smooth contour like the downs. The Pennines are greatest when you are among them, rather than pictures to admire from a respectful distance. There the huddle of the pikes or muddle of shapes takes form as well as colour. These resplendent heights are not so far from the cotton mills of Lancashire and the mines of Yorkshire and Durham. They are a thousand feet and more higher than the highest part of the Midland Railway, where it crosses the range on its way from Carlisle to Leeds; but even at Aisgill where the proud altitude is placarded by the railway managers, you are given a foretaste of the paradise of the industrial tourist which stretches away to the north.

Where the Pennines rise to their highest level, all the northern counties of Cumberland, Westmoreland, North-umberland, Durham and Yorkshire come close together. From that watershed flow little brooks that soon 'into glory peep'; the northern Tyne, starting due north, the Tees, on its way to form the boundary of Durham and Yorkshire, the Swale, preparing to cut out a vale 'lovelier than all the valleys of Ionian hills'. They are for the most part gentle enough but at High Four and Hardraw are cataracts which excel, in volume at any rate, any within the island. When, like the rivers, you come down from the high land into the great plain and proceed towards the sea, you become aware of a feature that Yorkshire shares with Somerset. The York wolds behind Whitby and the York moors behind Flam- borough Head, tilt their streams inland and keep their un- broken height till they are cut sheer into magnificent cliffs by the sea. The North Riding, which excels in acreage all the counties save two, is altogether unrivalled in succession of scenes, and the famous Richmond view from the upper river over the plain contains three quarters of these many attributes.

The southern part of the great range, down to the Peak of Derbyshire, has a quite distinct character. There is no false contrast as of the north and south Cotswolds. A native of the Peak has called the hills ' work-a-day', and it applies fitly to more than one aspect.

Industry, especially the textile industries, have laid long tapering fingers on the Pennine valleys. Away in the remote folds of the hills you come on small bleaching and dyeing works, built in the old unpretentious way with squared blocks of the gritstone; and in the long tortuous troughs of the main valleys are weaving villages with as many souls in them as a cathedral city in the plains. Nobody talks about 'the desecration of the countryside' in respect of these valleys; in part, perhaps, because it was all done so long ago, but most of all, because it is not a desecration at all, in the sense of bringing into the country an alien element which has no business there.

But the quality of the country goes deeper than these man-made accretions, however consonant they may be with its nature. The very stuff of which it is made has the character of honest labour about it. The millstone grit, as its name proclaims, is a rock made to work for its living; and even the word 'grit' brings at once to the mind the idea of courage and determination in adversity.

Not, of course, that the whole country is made of millstone grit. The true rock occurs only in comparatively thin layers, between bigger thicknesses of shales and inferior grits and sandstones. But wherever it crops out, it dominates the scene. Its small frowning escarpments give definition, almost shapeliness, to what might otherwise be merely long, tedious gradients. And where it gets the surface of the earth to itself, in places where the gradient of the hill coincides with the dip of the strata, so that the grit, having got on top, stays on top for miles at a time, it produces a kind of country which occurs nowhere else, the country of Stanage Edge and the Hallam moors, where the brown tussocky moorland goes on building itself up by an infinitely constant and deliberate process to a tremendous climax of downward plunge and spacious revelation, like a life lived all through for one tremendous moment of dedication and achievement.

Perhaps it is an inflation to speak this way of the comparatively modest ups and downs in scale of the Peak country. After all, there are here no Scafell Crags, nothing like the Ogwen face of the Glyders or any face of the Cuillins. But one does not feel the gritstone crags to be insignificant when one is with them. And besides, they have done their own work, made their own way in life.

The imposing precipices that inspire the big mountains owe their existence largely to the glaciers of the Ice Age which scooped out the cwms and combes over which they swagger. But the glaciers have left little mark on the Peak. The streams of ice impinged on its western flank, carrying their load of boulders of Shap granite, or red sandstone from the Cheviot, through the lowlands of Lancashire and Cheshire. But the Peak, too high to submit to the main body of the invasion, yet not high enough to generate serious glaciers of its own, escaped the violent masterful process of erosion, which gave us Cwm Dyli and the Garbh Coire on Braeriach and the Patterdale side of Helvellyn. The millstone grit has had to work its way through by the milder processes of wind and rain; and it has done itself credit. Stanage and Kinder Downfall and the Staffordshire Roaches are things to be proud of in any country or in any company.

But no doubt it is a mark of rockclimbers' snobbery to think about mountain scenery so much in terms of its precipices. They may be the most conspicuous features of the landscape, but they are not all of it; the vertical is only one element in form. The infinitely various diagonals play possibly a larger part. And it is here that the rather less resistant rocks score. For the water which has been the main agent in shaping the Peak has been able to eat down through these, scouring deep valleys, the flanks of which alternate effectively between crag, great steepness and gentler slopes where erosion has encountered a band of tougher material.

Probably the natural form for the wall of a mountain valley to take, if the material is homogeneous, is the convex, steepest at the foot, where the stream is most active, less so higher up where side streams and landslips try vainly to keep pace in the work of excavation. But this form is not the most effective in appearance. The steep lower slope either masks (when seen from below) the upper part and so detracts from the apparent height of the whole, or (if the spectator is above) disappears altogether.

But where you have a slope alternately steep and gentle, or steep above rising out of a more moderate convex slope, then you have a much finer effect, like the body emerging from a crinoline, which is the most beautiful and imposing form of costume yet devised by the mind of man.

This effect you have often in the Peak and in the moor-land country lying to the north of it. On top, the tough grit has acted as a shield and prevented the weather from eating the whole lump away. Below its brief escarpment, say fifty feet of dark vertical gritstone, comes a long steep slope, covered with rough grass and bilberries and strewn with boulders from the overlying rock; this is where the soft layers have yielded to erosion. Then comes a swelling breast as a harder layer impedes the erosive process but can-not quite withstand it. You hardly ever see a run of scree in grit country. If the grit gets broken up into such small pieces as make scree, it will disintegrate entirely and go back into earth. And finally the stream will cut itself yet another abrupt inner gorge as it strikes a softer layer again.

You will see a fine illustration of this all along the northern face of Kinder Scout, which is the highest hill in

the district, and in the whole Pennine range south of the
Craven fault. If you look up Ashop Clough from the
Snake Inn, you will see on top of all the rocky fringe called
emphatically 'The Edge', as if to say that no other counts
when it is in view. Then follows a very steep grassy slope of
400 feet or so, billowing out into the suave gradients of
Black Ashop Moor. And then again the land falls abruptly
into the trough of the Ashop.

A little further east, the figure is repeated, with Seal
Flats and the Wicken sustaining the plunge which comes
down from Seal Edge; and east again, the broad shoulders
of Dean Hill both sustain the plunge from Blackdean Edge
and themselves plunge into the Ashop at Blackdean Barn.

I have spoken already of the other form which is most
characteristic of the Peak—the long slow rise toppling over
into a tremendous fall. One sees this to the best advantage
on the east side of the district, on the Yorkshire edges; and
there it is enhanced by the fact that two layers of the true
grit overlie each other, and so you get a double rise and fall.
Follow the Derwent down from its lonely springs on the
Howden moors as far as Baslow. The whole way, the
double edge (sometimes a little disjointed) lowers over it. In
the northern part of the course, it is the upper tier which has
shape and bold definition—the fantastically wind-sculp-
tured blocks of Derwent Edge, like any trimmed box trees;
then the four mile rock ribbon of Stanage, perhaps the
finest continuous crag in the district; then the milder grass
—and heather—grown brow of White Edge, with little
Gardom's Edge as a last fling. Conversely, the lower tier
starts fairly tamely with a steep bank above the Derwent and

Plate 27. The Moors, from Kinderscout

gains confidence as it goes south, through the ragged wall of Bamford Edge to the clean tough ramparts of Froggatt Edge and Curbar Edge.

Without going over to the Yorkshire side, the traveller between Lancashire and London by the Midland line will notice a splendid instance of the double tier just as the train goes through Chinley, in Chinley Churn (? cairn; but cairn is a Celtic usage, remote from this country) and Cracken Edge. The latter is not rocky, but the sheerest pitch of grass. And even the imperious Roaches, far down in the Staffordshire corner have a less conspicuous lower tier running submissively below them.

And what lies over and above these formidable declivities? Few but those born to it relish the characteristic blend of peat, gravel, tussocks, heather, bilberries and cotton grass which carpets the upper flats of these moors. The peat is dominant, whether naked and trenched into slippery-sided 'groughs' as it is on Kinder Scout and Bleaklow, or veiled in still growing plants, soon to be converted into peat in their turn, as you may see it on Margery Hill above the Derwent. Some find it not only tedious but repulsive and even terrifying. Standing on a grey autumn day by the Kinder Downfall, with spray blowing up the swarthy rocks before him, and behind the leagues of barren brown peat rising and falling like the waves of a choppy sea, a visitor said with some fervency that it put him in mind of Dante's *Inferno*, if Hell were cold.

On moors not quite so high and bare, and especially a bit further north, in Lancashire and on the Yorkshire borders, the ground is less savage and is often exquisitely

coloured in a subdued way with the bright foliage of bil-
berry peering through the more sombre grasses. Walking
the lonely ridge which goes south from Blackstone Edge,
one is astonished at its warm, exciting colour, even on a
sullen, rainy day.

There is little that is savage about the lower skirts of the
hills. Where they excel is in quiet, pastoral quality. This
quality is most abundant on the west side of the country,
the Cheshire borders. For in the valleys here is all that you
could wish of green meadows and blooming hedgerows—
there are no prettier hedges than in Combs valley when the
foul-cherry is in flower—and the brooks run stronger and
cleaner than those of the south country. But there is something beyond this, a sense not of parsimony but of frugality,
an almost deliberately simple note, which eschews the
softer and more sensuous aids to beauty. The land is never
opulent; there is none of the cloying sweetness of the
Cheshire dairying acres which these western outposts of
the Peak overlook; the few parks here seem alien and
exotic.

The country is not lacking in trees, but they do not serve
here to give it, as in some other parts, a more domesticated
look. It is perhaps because they grow, or have been planted
so often, on exceedingly steep slopes, from which they
derive a kind of wild defiance, like the bard crying, 'Ruin
seize thee, ruthless king,' in Gray's ode. Only in the woods
near Hathersage can one find any of that quiet, reassuring
beauty which draws one to the woodlands of, say, the
Chilterns or the Midland spinneys. The forests of the Goyt
and the Dane—or what remains of them—breathe a more

savage and distrustful air, though the rivers are amenable enough.

The real heart of the Peak is the great limestone plateau which fills the southern centre of the district, and the gorges which intersect it.

It has been left aside until now, because it seems so utterly different in character to the rest of the country that it would be simply confusing to try to write about the two under one head; as despairing novel reviewers confound their readers by trying to discern some common element in the week's batch of new books. It is queer stuff, this mountain lime-stone. Wherever it pops up, it is true to its own kind and completely indifferent to its surroundings. You spot it at once, just as you can spot 'theatricals' in a small-town hotel. Whether in the Peak or in Craven or on the fringes of the Lake District or bordering the Silurian in North Wales or the Old Red Sandstone in South Wales, or in the Men-dips, the mountain limestone keeps itself to itself as if it was imbued with a kind of caste feeling.

But there is this to be said of the limestone country of the Peak; it is more compact and self-sustaining than any other of its sort in England. It does not fawn upon its neighbours. You might live a lifetime on these suave uplands, pale, arid, flecked with spots of white rock which give them an air not so much feminine as effeminate, without ever coming to think that there was another darker, wetter world outside.

Here, too, is a special point about the limestone part of the Peak. The valleys are for the most part too narrow to be inhabited. Dove Dale, Wye Dale, Lathkill Dale, the gorges of the Manifold and the Hamps, are mere slits in the

Plate 28. In the Derwent Valley

face of the earth, and you cannot always be sure even of finding water at the bottom of them. They are beautiful to walk down, but you cannot live in them. And in this respect does the white country differ most from all else in the Peak—that you can find in these dales something which is clean away from the workaday world, which is of no *use* to anyone (except a few fishing men whose prerogative in the streams is jealously preserved) and which is good only to look at and to wonder at. It is right that there should be such places; it's a poor world without its courtesans. And that, I suppose, is why a million have heard of, or even seen, Dove Dale for every hundred who know the Derwent and the Dane.

Not that Dove Dale is unworthy of the mark which she has made on the world. At her best, there is no such place to be found in the length and breadth of Britain. No other has such sustained pictorial quality, such a changing variety of bluffs and pinnacles and flying buttresses, such a rich embroidery of thickets and flowers blooming in all seasons, so that the dale is never without a gleam of bright colour all the summer long. The river itself is to some a little disap-pointing. It has seemed a bit tame and on occasion even muddied and sordid, in the midst of all the magnificence it has gathered round it. But that is the way with a courtesan of a river.

There is no room here to speak of Dove Dale's more virtuous and less opulent sisters, as Chee Dale, in some ways the finer-featured of the two, and Lathkill Dale, the most intimate in its charm. But a word must be said for the uplands, which many have dismissed as dull and shapeless, but which to others are full of subtle effects of contour and colour.

It is an extraordinarily open-hearted country; there is in it nothing private and secretive. It has ups and downs but none so considerable that it loses touch with its neighbouring acres; like Mr. Bernard Shaw's definition of a Socialist state as one in which no one would be so rich or so poor that he could feel he was marrying beneath or above his station. It has no woods. Its trees are clumps of wind-swept beeches, planted to shelter a farm or to mark a swelling breast of downland. It has no comfortable hedges. Its stone walls are white and chequer the green in vivid patterns. The farms and villages are a luminous grey-white. A faint air of mystery and somehow supernatural light hangs over it all.

No one who is new to the country should fail to visit Edale (even if there is a threat to strike oil there) and to walk along the ridge of Mam Tor, Back Tor and Lose Hill, which juts out into space like the pirates' frisky plank, and commands at once the south flank of Kinder Scout (representing the gritstone) and the Castleton moors (where the limestone begins).

With regard to Dove Dale, it is a splendid day to follow the river all the way from its source to Thorpe or Ashbourne. But a still better day is to follow the Wye down from Buxton to Millersdale, then south over the plateau to Monyash, and down Lathkill Dale to Bakewell; this will give you the white country both high and low.

Of all the moorland ridges, none is better worth a visit than Derwent Edge, but not when the grouse are nesting, for then it is jealously guarded; and of all the rivers, none is

more kindly and gracious than the well-forested Dane. For
a close-set park-like elegance, there is nothing to beat High-
low Brook and Abney Clough; for a green pastoral, there
is the valley of the Todd Brook above Whaley Bridge. And
when summer is young and the bluebells are out, Hebden
Water can hold its own with anything in the Peak proper.

Ashopton is the prettiest of all confluences, but this the
envious water engineers must soon steal from us.

CHAPTER XII

The Lakes

England is broad-based in a physical as well as the moral sense of which Tennyson wrote. It narrows from south to north; and our mental attitude as well as our map-makers compel us to regard the north as the top. In spite of the absolute smallness of the island you have in the south a sense of quiet and unhampered space. Joy is unconfined. As you reach the northern counties the feeling of the country is utterly and entirely different. We may imagine England to have been cut out of a rectangle of stuff which was pinched into crumples at the top, as one squeezes the mouth of a paper bag. The sharp ridges so formed spread into wider, flatter, less definite shapes southward of the pinching point, but remained sharp and firm at the top. The Pennines, the Cheviots, and the Cumberland hills are among the sharp-est and highest edges.

The contraction of England in the north is enhanced by the influence of its industries. Scores of big industrial towns are wedged into the narrow space, with the roads and rail-ways that are their necessary accompaniment. On the western side the sea is often difficult of approach. Its shore is cantankerous. The first electric railway in the country was built to join Liverpool with Southport. Both of these towns are almost on the sea—but not quite. At Southport, a place famous for its flowers, everyone looks for the sea but cannot find it. The railway feeds a succession of links, beautiful in themselves as well as for the game of golf; but they, too, are cut from the sea by difficult dunes. The immense, the almost notorious popularity of the northern Blackpool (there is also a Blackpool in Devon) is due in the first instance to the rare accessibility of its beach. In this region it is a surprise to find a wide space (on the west of Blundellsands) that resembles the East Anglian Fens; a black soil region often kept fit for its rich crops of potatoes and grain by very deep dykes which are found in the woodlands (surviving from days when King John kept a special forester there) and in the fields of country houses as well as on wider fields. Mallard and teal, woodcock and snipe are numerous almost among the houses of Liverpool's spreading suburbs. Hares abound, some of them 'escapes' from the flat and ample plain of Aintree where the Waterloo Cup for greyhounds is run. Throughout Lancashire, though its agriculture is as good as the best in England, and as various, the population is vast. The towns are many and large; and the buildings in general more conspicuous for use than beauty. It has been pointed out that one of the chief Roman forts and camps in the region was built at the very hub of the railway system of Manchester. The towns have wiped out the country scene and past history, or so you might think. Yet the outstanding marvel of the country—in Yorkshire, Durham and Northumberland, as well as in Lancashire, Westmorland and Cumberland—is the contiguity of country spaces that are among the wildest, the least spoiled, and the most thinly populated within the island.

Barrow-in-Furness is as good an example as any. It may

almost be called a gateway to the Lakes, a grim warder
enough to the realm of romance and poetry, an unlikely
ante-chamber to the high loneliness of Helvellyn and Scafell, whose very names are eloquent of their wild nature to
all dwellers in the north. Such industrial ante-chambers are
crowded with men and women who thirst for the wildness,
the romance, the poetry of unsullied country. It is so in
Derby, in Lancashire, and not least in Yorkshire. 'The
Peak' (as if there were no other), the Lakes, the Pennines
keep romance alive, and have earned a repute that is in part
due to the gratitude of crowded population at their doors.
Their native wildness and inherent beauty are enhanced by
the crush of life just outside their pale. The Peak of Derbyshire is unbelievably small to those whose intimate know-
ledge of it is confronted with statistical figures. The Lakes
themselves are a little like Milton's emmet—'in small room
large heart enclosed'. Both contain the very essence of
romantic scenery and give the sense of being 'wrapt from
the world' and 'aloof from its mutations and unrest'. Both
have a much stronger justification for the definite article of
their title than 'the Shires'. They remain to thousands, to
millions, 'The Peak' and 'The Lakes'.

The Lakes possess a virtue that is not seen elsewhere in so
high a power. Their climate is such that the light shifts and
varies not only quickly but to extremes; and the lakes themselves nurse and reflect these bouts of lightness and darkness, of mist and candour as a face responds to emotion.
We all know how Constable, painting in the neighbourhood of his Flatford Mill in Suffolk, could transfigure a
scene by the agency of a rainbow. Scenes in the Lakes are

yet more emphatically changed by sun shining on rain or succeeding it. In the hilly but rather waterless island of Madeira a rainbow will last throughout a good part of the day, because it is painted on the canvas of a mist that passes continuously through a pass in the hills. The rainbows of the Lakes are more splendid and much less calculable. They compose transformation scenes with a mystic suddenness. They seem to suck their splendour from the weight of the rain, which in most months of the year has a certain likeness to the April shower, sudden and bright, seldom slow and sulky. You may live in the Lakes and never see the same view twice.

Few features in nature are less fitful in mood and colour than a deep mountain tarn closely encircled by dark walls. It may look like a solid thing, black as a pool of asphalt; and even the reflections look as if they were graven. These Cumbrian and Westmorland lakes, with one or two exceptions, are of a contrary character to the pool or upper tarn. Their usual nature is to change like the light that half reveals and half conceals their living waters.

Their species is worth some emphasis. Now it is a common habit among owners of country houses in the south of England to dam the little streams where they flow through their property to the end of making a wide ornamental water. Good examples are at Luton Hoo and Brocket on the Lea and Tewin on the Maram. These artificial valley lakes are in one aspect imitations of the lakes of Westmorland and Cumberland, which as a rule are formed by the flowing of a river into a cup in the hills; and it is a part of their character to keep the quality of both lake and stream. They are long

L

Plate 29. Springtime in the Lakes, looking towards Scafell

and not very broad, belonging to the upper valleys where
their home is. They are not at all of the nature of tarns or
pools giving a sense of stagnation. Though we speak of the
Lakes, many of them individually are known as Waters.
They are organic to the lofty watershed from which they
radiate. They have been compared to the spokes of a wheel,
a metaphor very ingeniously worked out by Mr. Carton in
his *England*. There is the hub of the hills. The clouds bombard it, as the waves bombard the coast, and comb out the
waters. Some of the higher peaks have a hundred inches
more of rain than any part of Essex. The rain from heaven
meets rocky springs, and the streams are born nearer to the
peaks than in most districts and so begin to carve the valleys
and delve hollows for their own waters. This natural lake is
the model of the engineers who have created greater lakes at
a considerable altitude for the provision of water for the
great towns. The northern reservoirs differ from the immense and very lovely lakes in the Elan Valley by the
greater activity of the afforesters who have clothed the walls
of the lakes with thickly planted conifers. Such woods have
their place; and their value is not only economic; but the
method of symmetric planting of fir and pine has spread so
widely as to distress many lovers of lake scenery. A fir wood
might look comely enough on a hillside and seem in keeping with the place, if it were not geometrically planned. In
the wild naturalness of the lakes a formal pattern is wholly
offensive and out of place.

The mechanical damming of water is seldom to be de-
plored, aesthetically. There is a very characteristic hillside a
few miles north of Kendal, a proper gateway to the Lakes,

down which trickles a wandering stream that may some/
times be heard and not seen, so much does it undercut the
coherent roots of the peaty grasses. As soon as you leave the
last houses and cultivated fields you are wading among
bracken and the hummocks of the grass and may listen
without interruption to the 'music born of murmuring
sound'. Progress is slow, but at each step the feeling of
aloofness increases, and whenever you look back the ex/
panse of the distant view widens. You are not in the wilder
and more famous part of the Lakes, but wish for nothing
better. Quite suddenly as you turn to descend by a different
route to the little hamlet you have left, you come upon a
duck pool: a small burn has been banked up to provide
water power for a farmer and for a little factory; all is natural
and desirable. Indeed the harnessing of water for power
might have been done for the sake of the view. There is a
water/wheel beside a little spinning and weaving factory in
a south Welsh valley near Solva that is worth a visit for its
own sake: it sets a flourish on the kindly valley. So it is in
Westmorland. Even a factory may be a thing of beauty, if it
is rightly conceived.

Many parts of the Lake District are quiet, green and rest/
ful, like southern valleys. Those who gather in their multi/
tude to watch the hounds' trail or the working sheep dogs
in the neighbourhood of Rydal, might almost be at a sheep/
dog trial in Hatfield Park, except for the greater space and
higher slopes. The quality of the scene is not mountainous
or riverine. It is made by trees and green grass and bracken
and delicate undulations. You know but would hardly
infer that this was the breeding centre of the sheep dog

which will rove at a word to distant and difficult places
to recover a lost sheep. Yet the sheep dogs are like a native
fauna (as once were the wild cats); and that unexpected
oddity in many of the best (which have one blue and one
dark eye) belongs to the region. They and their shepherds
are an attribute of the hills. Hereabouts is the Wordsworth
who felt that he had discovered the lesser celandine, not the
Wordsworth whom the cataract 'haunted like a passion'.
With regard to that same humble flower, it is perhaps an
indication that it is more characteristic of the south than the
north that the plaque to Wordsworth's memory in the
Rydal Church is carved not with the lesser but the greater
celandine, which is a plant of a very different species, probably an 'escape' from gardens.

What exactly are 'the Lakes'? The region, unlike most
others within the island, is definite enough to demand a
special name. It is a hilly region of about thirty miles by
twenty-five; longer from north to south than from east to
west, which lies, as to a minute fraction, towards Furness,
in Lancashire, but for the rest occupies a good part of both
Westmorland and Cumberland. It is more or less 'ribbed
and paled in' by limestone, but its ruggeder heights consist
of hard slates and of granite. Scafell Pike, which rises to
three thousand two hundred and ten feet, is supreme over
all other peaks or tops in the island. It has no approximate
peer. It may be said to resemble a central tent-pole from
which descend in deep folds the canvas of the most
glorious part of the Lake country. If you look at it on a
coloured map that emphasises physical qualities, it suggests the head of a Medusa from which descend a number

of writhing snakes or suckers. The comparison does more justice to the queerly crooked lines of the river-lake than the standard likeness to the hub of a wheel. The view from the Pike itself suggests no likeness to any set pattern. It is a magnificent tumble of hill and watered valleys, wild and tremendous, beyond all other prospects. Of course not the whole of the region of the Lakes does depend from Scafell and its neighbour peaks; but these are the essential core, the citadel of the magnificence. Many little tarns exist above the seventeen or so larger lakes; and a census of such features of the scenery would vary at different seasons and according to the rainfall. When rains are very heavy a wide lake, as in Borrowdale, may supplant a marsh or lowland meadow.

Scafell has a geographical supremacy; but it does not coincide with the aesthetic centre of the district. Who shall decide where the heart of the landscape lies? Windermere has passed on its name to the most pleasing of all the warmer and snugger valleys of the Canadian Selkirks; and it has a world-wide name. Ambleside, towards the northern point of it, is known to thousands of tourists and well deserves its popularity, though perhaps those who live in the Lakes and are familiar with its recesses will hardly endorse the popular verdict. Windermere is very much the largest of the lakes and for that reason, it may be, less full of surprises than other smaller lakes, especially those to the west; but its nature and its proportions make a text-book of the attributes of the region. It is ten miles in length and less than two miles across in the broader part. It is of the river riverine, a fresh and flowing piece of water, with no suggestion at any season of grim stagnancy. Yet how the scene varies, even from hour to hour. The rainfall of the Lake District is almost a byword, but it is due to the weight of the individual showers more than the continuance of the fall. The hills are blotted out, the lake almost boils. Then, before you know it, the sun is out and the ridges—especially in this regard Helvellyn—appear with a razor edge. Stone walls and wandering sheep are distinct as printed matter; and the hillsides reassume their seasonal colour. The next day the outlines of the hills may be soft and vague or 'clothed in white samite, mystic, wonderful'; and patches of the lower slopes gleam and darken as 'the clouds the clouds chase'. You may climb a hill one day and regard the pleasurable toil as almost a domestic amusement. The next you may be caught with fears and risk a long and dangerous exposure. The atmosphere is continually making and unmaking the scene to the eye, as the rains may swell the old lakes and create a new one.

Windermere is many miles inland; and its votaries are apt to disregard the sea, to be wholly content with the 'inland murmur'. The district is alone among neighbours of the sea in satisfying its visitors with fresh water instead of salt. Yet the coast from Morecambe Bay northwards is magnificent, carved into deeply cut patterns by both the streams and the Atlantic waves. No town or centre in north England rivals Glasgow from which the Clyde floats you down to a delectable shore and a host of wild and various islands. Its very slums are an ante-room to lochs and islands of a high romance and a spacious fame. The western boundary of the Lakes is not so obviously accessible,

and to thousands of visitors it is barred off by the moun‚
tains; but they miss some of the grandest prospects within
Britain. Morecambe Bay and the inlets and rocks
north of it are a worthy approach and introduction to the
surroundings of the mouth of the Clyde and the Solway
Firth.

There are many ways of seeing a country. You may fly
over; and two of the most genuine and most ingenious
descriptions of England known to the writer were written
by American and German airmen. The American's first
impression of this strange neat quiet green land was inspired
by the scene from the train window when he first landed;
and his later flights, in preparation for the war, confirmed
his first admiration. The Germans wrote after an enforced
drift in a balloon across England from east to west. Their
verdict was much the same as the American's; the land
seemed to be a land smiling with continuous gardens and
snug hamlets.

The mosaic of a closely settled country makes the best
view from the air, for the angle of vision flattens hills and
building. The lofty spire of Salisbury, for example, is
dwarfed to a point. A glorious mountain landscape may be
almost dull; but the Lakes are an exception. The silver
bands of water in their quaint pattern stand out in bright
distinction and the contiguity of the sea is emphasised.

You may see the Lakes with surprising intimacy from a
motor‚car; and it is the special quality of observation from
a car on a road that you appreciate the general lie of the
land. It is an education, for example, in geology as well as
topography to cross the Weald of Kent from the Hog's

Back to Hastings, or to descend from the Mendips into willow-lined marsh-meadows of Somerset. There are fine views—and always indications of fine views—from the trains that take you to Kendal or Carlisle, but you are all the while a peri outside Paradise desiring, but as yet forbidden entry through the gate.

If you leave the train for a motor-car you are not vouchsafed, as in southern England, a quick or comprehensive view of the structural basis of the land; but almost like a walker you may come close to the heart of the scene. You may do this; but you are often warned not to. It is no unfamiliar experience to pass a burnt-out car or the signs of its extinction at the side of the road. On minor roads the ascent may be nearly one in four. The routes from Ambleside to Buttermere are very long or rather short and the longest way round is certainly the quickest way home though none the less glorious. Yet you cannot discover the true character of the Lakes, or of any other place, except from your feet or in Cobbett's way, from the back of a horse; and the horse will often be defeated. For example, one of the oldest and most famous, if smallest and cheapest, fox-hunts within the country is the Blencathra. In the shires the hunt is the most evanescent of scenes for any pedestrian, though hunting by motor-car has become so popular as to be a hindrance to the sport. In some of the Cumberland and the Westmorland hunts, a walker who is wise enough to gain a certain altitude before the day begins, may share in the sport, if he is lucky, till the hounds go home. They themselves are a product of the country, strong, short-limbed and perhaps much keener in scent than the tall cat-footed hounds which win prizes at the Peterboro' Show. The foxes make no distant points, but cling to the cover of their native rocks.

Some of the roads against which motorists are warned compel a certain degree of walking. They may pass through the gates of a farmhouse or even end in a slate quarry.

The railways, choosing the valley, help to define the Lake District and it is singularly capable of definition. Between north-east and north-west England, in spite of their contiguity in a narrow space, a great gulf is fixed; and there is one bridge north of the Peak of Derbyshire. Carlisle, as much for historical as geographical reasons, may be said to guard the Lakes in the north as Kendal on the south-east. The valley up which runs the railway, always giving gracious views, completely severs these groups of hills and lakes from the eastern part of this narrow piece of England. There are two countries within it, both glorious with hills; but the Pennines, of the eastern half, and Scafell or Helvellyn on the west bear curiously little likeness to one another in scenic essentials.

Within the charmed circle of the Lakes one thinks first of all of lake and hill; and scarcely of rivers; but as you come towards this dividing gulf rivers take their proper place again. The Lune, by Kirby Lonsdale for example, has here and there cut out banks of a form and colour not found in combination elsewhere. Through the great landscape garden of one country house it flows at the foot of a steep cliff of red sandstone on one side with lowland on the other. The cliff is broken enough to encourage tree and bush; and the natural vegetation has been advantaged by the planting of bushes of barberry and many other coloured shrubs which compete gloriously with the protruding boulders of the ruddy stone on which the scene is built. High bridges of a single arch (such as the new artists in concrete have successfully exaggerated at Oxford and elsewhere) frame green and pleasant views reflected in perfection in the smoother reaches. We are miles away from the small tumbling streams of the centre of the Lake District; but there is this in common between the river in the plain and the burn on the hillside, that they nurse the same wild life. The trout abound and so do the otters. It may perhaps be usefully put on record in this regard that some of the most ardent fishermen delight in the presence of otters; and in Westmorland lives one owner of a long piece of a trout stream, who takes definite steps to encourage the otters. He believes that they are agents in the work of ensuring the survival of the fittest. Their victims are weak and diseased fish, and the various creatures that destroy the spawn of fish. That quaint and pleasing bird, the dipper, which is at home even under the water, abounds; and in gardens thereabouts the smallest and brightest of all our birds, the golden-crested wren, may be as plentiful and nearly as tame as white butterflies on a cabbage patch.

The Lakes come nearest, in distance as in character, to other hills of a more eastern character and association, near Kirby Lonsdale where the Lune has had a hilly passage on its way to the Irish Channel. A greater gulf between east and west has its central depth in the river Eden with road and rail fitfully obedient to its course. It is chiefly the incidence of this long fair valley running from south to north along the enlarging river that isolates the Lakes and carves out a unit that has no other likeness. The Lakes are a moated fortress of many towers with angled walls that Vauban might have envied. The sea makes an easily de-fensible arc, in spite of the small successive estuaries, on the west; and the deep bracket of Morecambe Bay makes a curiously sharp intrusive angle to the south. The north is valley land, but just beyond is one of the greatest of all our inlets.

The brief Lune and the long Eden complete the fortress character to the east. No part of England—not the Shires, the Weald, the Hampshire basin or Snowdonia, not even the Cotswolds or the Fens, justify a single title so completely as the Lakes.

The district exports some of its aesthetic products. Cum-berland and Westmorland stone have a greater subtlety of tint and tissue than even the stone that is the making of the Cotswold village. It is more conspicuous in the walls on the hillside, which escape the gloom of some of the York-shire walls, than in the architecture of the district; and this is natural, for the Lakes give an added pleasure to the hordes of visitors because they are thinly populated. They possess a wildness rare within the island. This same stone has pleased so many eyes that it is quarried for a thousand gardens even in the far south. It possesses a peculiar affinity for lowly flower and leaf and a large stone may weather into the likeness of a miniature landscape.

Everyone has heard sung the delight of the soft sweet grass of the Southern Downs; but the only grass that is worth a high price and is carried afar is the Cumberland grass that takes so sweetly the bias of the box bowl. It is as precious as

a rare wood; and when you come upon it in its native
haunt you feel that neither Turk nor Persian ever compounded so firm and soft a carpet.

It would be a false and foolish comparison to argue that
one lake, one group of hills, one upland valley was superior
to another; but those miss the meaning of some of the
grandest passages of description and natural philosophy in
the language who have not visited the Wordsworth country and kept Wordsworth in their mind. Grasmere is Grasmere; but when you see the quiet snugness of Wordsworth's
cottage house you know that Wordsworth's inspiration
came in long walks; and only the walker can find out the
inner virtues. One of the best of special pleas has been
written by Mr. Walpole, an alien captured and enslaved by
the place in which he was chiefly immured, especially the
little hill of Cathell's 'which you can climb in twenty
minutes and then walk on "tops" for hours without effort,
carried on that springing turf as though with wings'. He
has also wider preferences. 'For myself,' he wrote in *English
Country*, 'Skiddaw, the Langdales, the Screes and Great
Gable are nearest my heart. I have never been on the top of
the Screes but I have been in front, behind, at the side. I
have seen their precipitous frowning surface glitter in the
sun like fireworks (with the crackling, sparkling fierceness
of fire). I have seen them so black that it was as though the
whole of Wasdale gritted its teeth with rage, and, only last
summer, I picknicked on the banks of Wastwater when,
through the heat-haze, they were unsubstantial like gos-
samer, with no weight, no substance. . . . Gable is not
always wet. I have had finer views from the top of it than

from anywhere else in the world. Again the contrast, the intimacy, the burning glittering belt of the sea and lakes everywhere, pools of light framed in ebony; immediately below, the Screes, like the black hilt of a knife cutting the green valley.' He dislikes the Coniston Old Man, because he was once lost on its face and slithered dangerously on its shale in a hostile and pursuing wind. Helvellyn can be frightening in like manner and indeed any 'Edge', where the shale is at the surface. The Lakes are not a test for climbers, but many of the hills must be taken seriously, even though no mist or rain blot out the world and the winds are still. There is no false wildness about the peaks and ridges. That abrupt volcanic emergence at Ambleside where many are first introduced to the Lakes is evidence enough of the nature of the hills.

In most parts of England the scene has been manu-factured, if the ugly word is allowable, by English people within the last two hundred years. The maintenance of the character depends on continuous work. Neither village nor hedge remains without continual care. This means that the scene is always vulnerable; *corruptio optimi pessima*, and the human scene may become the very devil, if the people do not continue in the active work of making and remak-ing England as a rainbow is remade at every instant. You cannot preserve England, negatively. The continuance of its charm implies continuous affection. The Lakes are in a different class. Though house and wall, homestead and sheep influence the beauty, the hills and lakes are the essen-tial. They remain almost as nature made them—in a matrix that was broken up and not repeated. The better part of that small but marvellous circle of some 7000 square miles can be preserved by the simple negative method of non-interference. Of all the humanised parts of the landscape, save the signs of the shepherd and his dog, the best is the great stone circle in the valley of Keswick under the Shoulder. The north-west corner where industrial scars begin is the one real exception.

As a matter of history the Lakes have been more free from desecration than most other districts, from 'ribbon development', and the sudden outcrop of 'concrete mendacities'. The seekers of health and beauty who have flocked into the circle have found in full force the blessed change they sought. A wild and natural glory, of a rare and satisfying pattern, has enveloped them after a few hours' journey from the presence of the grim trappings of industrial toil. A playground indeed was almost at their doors. They might have travelled the world and found no rarer scene.

Occasional local outrages there were; but in general all was well, until in 1924 the National Forestry Commission bought some seven thousand acres of the Hardknott Estate by Eskdale and Donnerdale, and presently began to plant severely regimented woods of conifers. Years earlier Wordsworth had made an almost venomous protest against the introduction of the alien greenness of the larch. Not a great number of people will agree with him: Britain is decorated with scores of alien trees, most of them beautiful. The Scotch pine, the spruce and the yew belong of right to the island but find suitable enough companions in other conifers and evergreens, including the larch. Yet it was true that some patches of larch interfered with the spirit of the scene that was his life-blood to Wordsworth; and almost every fir or pine plantation set in straight lines is distasteful. The Lakes are such an epitome of the wilder prospects for which the teeming populations at their edge yearn, they are so complete an inspiration for those who dwell there, that they should be the last place chosen for such an experiment.

Some of the most sacrosanct bits belong to the National Trust—and are happily safe in perpetuity—but it is not a question of partial preservation. The whole has a gracious unity of its own and is of a character wholly unparalleled in Britain or perhaps anywhere in the world. The Lakes are the Lakes and must remain as the Lake poets knew them. They are a national monument as well as a scene.

CHAPTER XIII

Park and Seaboard

One may scarcely think of the surface of North America or South Africa without giving a certain pre-eminence to the National Parks, to Banff, to the Yellowstone and Kruger Parks. They are placed where the scene is wild and magnificent. They are homes of wild beasts, of bear and bison and lion and the rest. Their scale is immense. In Kruger Park about a thousand head of deer, zebra and, occasionally, giraffe are killed every day by the lions alone. The national sanctuary is left to a nature that as ever is 'red in tooth and claw'.

The idea of the National Park has been transferred to Britain, by a sort of metaphor. It has been suggested that all sorts of places should be converted into National Parks: the Dales of Derby, the Lakes, the Forest of Dean, the New Forest, Exmoor, Dartmoor, Snowdonia, the Pembroke-shire coast. It may be doubted whether the phrase 'National Park' bears any meaning whatever in reference to such places. The ideas it conveys to different people are often contradictory. To some it means access for 'the public', to some sanctuary, from which necessarily the general public must be excluded. England has only one natural National Park, the seaside. Ownership, as things are, ceases below the half-tide mark. It would be no bad thing if it ceased well above high-water mark, so that no part of the British coast

was refused to Britons. The great headlands of the west coast fulfil the ideal of being wild and magnificent, and if they do not harbour wild beasts they are at least the home of great birds likely to be harried elsewhere: of peregrine falcon, of buzzard and raven and chough, with many gulls, and with grey seals. Lands End, Tintagel, Hartland Point, Baggy and Morte Points, St. David's Head, Great Orme's Head are all tremendous: they stand like buttresses of the nation's architecture. Some have been secured by the National Trust; but that Trust—so careless are we of our treasures—is not in any sense national. The nation as such does nothing whatever to endow or aid its efforts. If anyone desires the institution of a National Park he might begin by urging a comprehensive law for the preservation of the coast from domestic architecture, good or bad. A few districts there are, but very few, that have remained free enough from human habitation to be possible as parks or have the definition that a park requires. In England itself there are perhaps none in the south or east, and in the west only Dartmoor, Exmoor and the Lakes.

Snowdonia has a peculiar predominance. Snowdon itself is the highest mountain in the island outside Scotland. The mountain and those about it compose a single area of scenery of a wild splendour not repeated elsewhere. The antique rocks, singularly eloquent of glacial action, are a delight to geologists. On the heights grow flowers not found elsewhere. One of them is not found again till you reach the Caucasus. A flower sanctuary is urgently called for. The scene has all the elements of wildness that the people of a thickly populated island must desire. The little

M

Plate 30. Snowdon, from Plas Gwynant

lake below the Devil's Kitchen, against whose ascent
visitors are warned, is the mirror of a scene that should
remain for ever 'unspotted from the world'. Llanberis, at the
foot of Snowdon, the starting point of the primitive mountain railway, is not admirable as architecture but its site is
incomparable. The cascade though small as the world's
waterfalls go, might well haunt a poet 'like a passion'. The
twin lakes so narrowly joined together conclude a pass that
has no peer for wild beauty. Capel Curig is the doorway of
the most primal scene that even North Wales can give. The
sensitive may find ugly scars when they look over the lakes
to the sides of hills converted into bare vertical walls by the
quarrying of slate. A certain grandeur remains even in
those flattened walls, especially where pools deep and dark
have been formed at their base; but the quarries and the
architecture have doubtless maimed the organic glory of the
scene. Even at the topmost peak of Snowdon itself are a few
buildings that the eye desires to evade. Nevertheless the
greater part of Snowdonia can be salved, can be saved. The
mountains have been too strong for their enemies. One
precious morsel by the eastern approach to Snowdon is
already preserved in perpetuity. It is National Trust property. The Pass of Aberglaslyn is crucial. If there is any
wild and romantic scenery it is here where the two streams
meet at the edge of Beddgelert, where Llewellyn's faithful
hound is buried. The place is fathoms deep in Welsh history and romance; and every yard of the scene is eloquent of
its own influences. The rapid river, sometimes open, sometimes enveloped in trees, both deciduous and evergreen, the
hillsides that are sometimes precipices, the great enveloping

hills that make the Pass throughout its length a pass indeed, still breathe a spirit of wildness or, if you will, of unhuman-ised landscape that cannot be paralleled in England, not even in the Lakes, or for that matter in mountainous Wales itself. It might be spoilt. Excess of civilisation drives people into a passion for wildness; and some of them love wildness as Tom Tulliver was fond of birds, 'that is of throwing stones at them.' Their first inclination is to build house or shack or mountain railway. The scene might be spoilt, too, by mere private possession and the refusal of access. Some good might result from the conversion of all this district of Snowdonia—about the road from Beddgelert to Llanberis, about the river Glaslyn into a National Park—if one of the first steps in organising such a Park were the appointment of a Warden, who should be a keeper indeed. The public could not resent their exclusion from a little sanctuary or two for flowers or insects or birds. The little mountain rail-way that climbs the easier and duller side of Snowdon is no offence; and it is surprising how little it interferes with the cataract that falls at its feet.

There is another mountain railway in North Wales of a yet more primitive type that gives much finer views than the Snowdon track. It leads to the village of Blenau Festiniog. All the way up it opens new and gracious prospects into the deep valleys below the hillside along which it rises. A hillside garden as magnificent both in its views and its own riches as the more famous gardens above the Conway in Denbighshire, sidles up to one of the halts. So long as the railway rises, the views from the primitive rattling trucks are paradisal; but presently a more level reach is found and you

M2

are in the midst of houses that suggest every other type of ugliness that you associate with a mining village. If you would know how little regard for natural beauty has been felt by the pursuers of underground wealth, contrast Fes-tiniog and Blenau Festiniog. Mineral wealth must be pur-sued. We should not perhaps regret the mines or the vast slate quarries that have flattened the great hills above the lakes at Llanberis, but there is no reason why miners should live in uglier houses than other people.

All this region of North Wales is a proper place of pil-grimage for the world in general. It is a region for walkers and climbers. It responds to slow investigation as well as to a rapid survey. It may be hailed even as a distant cousin to Banff in the Rockies, if not to Kruger's Park; and doubtless if it were to become a National Park its vogue in the world at large would be greatly enhanced. Whether this is a con-summation to be desired is another question.

England has no region of any size that can compare with Snowdonia or rival its claim to be a National Park. Eng-land is dotted all over with sanctuaries; and may their numbers increase! Even Staffordshire has its sanctuary alongside one of the most popular haunts of the tripper. Close to its industrial centres, peaks and scoops are found not less well endowed with natural charms than the Dales of Derbyshire itself. Such quiet and well defined reserves for bird and plant and insect have no relationship with the Park, which needs wider and wilder spaces than are to be found. Omitting the Lakes, there are exactly two: Exmoor and Dartmoor. Out of the plains of Somerset the old sand-stone rocks rise to a surprising height almost to the sea's

edge; and at the higher levels cultivation becomes impossible, and trees cannot live. Walking through the heather
you will come upon endless seedlings of trees, especially
rowan, but none comes to maturity, partly, though not
wholly, because of the mere bleakness. In the very latest
account of the highest point on the moor it is suggested that
the prehistoric stones and other signs of population indicate
that Exmoor was once a place of refuge made safe by its
wild remoteness. It is more likely perhaps that here as on
the Cotswolds or the Berkshire and Hampshire downs, as
at Avebury and Stonehenge, the place was chosen because
it was free of forest. Exmoor is one of the few places where
that most splendid of our wild animals, the red deer, is
altogether at home; but the moor is too bleak for the deer
themselves in heavy wintry weather, and they descend to
the woods and the scooped valleys. It is a glorious place for
a man on a horse or even in a car. Dunkerry Beacon has a
wider sweep than any other of the beacons of western England. You may pick out on a day of high visibility the
Malvern hills, Brown Willy in Cornwall and the Brecon
Beacons across the Bristol Channel. It is precious even
among National Trust possessions. The bleakness of the
moor, where no trees grow, is approached by combes and
river valleys singularly soft and thickly treed. The Exe,
rising close to the sea, carves its lovely way through the edge
of Somerset and across the whole of Devon after the same
fashion as the Wye and the Severn. Exmoor is its Plin-
limmon. Travelling from the north or east you may circumvent Exmoor by the long valley that runs along the eastern
edge; but it is best to mount the hill through Dulverton.

You emerge upon the stark moor through woods that enjoy the soft warmth and miss the salted winds. Some sudden clefts there are which may be the death of horse and hound and even of the quarry they pursue, but for the most part the steep combes are as friendly as the valleys of Hampshire itself. The beginning of the valley of the Barbe, famous for the Tarre steps—a bridge of enormous stones placed there by a prehistoric folk—is as good an example as any of the making of a Devon combe. The mighty stones of the bridge are evidence of the nature of the stone that underlies the moor, as the roofs and walls of Cotswold cottages express their foundations. It is not always so. The mightiest and oldest monuments on the chalk downs are a greater engineering feat than even this bridge.

Dartmoor confesses its foundations more manifestly than Exmoor. The height is greater; indeed Dartmoor is the only high land in southern England that reaches two thousand feet, and so, as some reckon, deserves the name of mountain. Granite is of its essence; and great granite boulders as well as the solid rock are exposed. Their strength and solidity first suggested the right material for the building of the Eddystone Lighthouse. There have often been times when the builders have rejected the strongest native materials because of the labour involved in their shaping. After the Great War, oak for a little while was cheaper than pine for this reason; and granite has never been so popular even in the granite countries as limestones and sandstones. Though Dartmoor is the higher, Dunkerry Beacon has no close parallel, and its most famous resorts are rather the valleys and combes than the bleak hilltops. Widdicombe, which

like Dunkerry, belongs in part to the National Trust, comes
first, not from its fame in song only. It is old in art as in
nature. It is sheltered, but on the edge of utter bleakness. It
is remote, but easily approached and a good point for
excursion into the precipitous moors. The Church House,
of course, is a real historic monument. One reason why
the lower levels of Dartmoor are of more account than
the peaks—even than Yes Tor, is that they are more precipitous. Some geologists, letting their imagination free,
have suggested that Dartmoor is the one place where the
scenery is much of the same nature as it was a while after
'the great upheaval' when the molten granite first cooled
and set. Geology, which is the geography of the past, is here
also the geography of the present. However that may be—
and it is a plausible theory—there is reason to believe that
rain impregnated with vegetable chemicals, is more de-
structive than unadulterated rain. Its mechanical hammering at the harder type of granite is a vain nagging; yet its
slow soaking may disintegrate all sorts of stone and reduce
them almost to the consistency of a rotten oak bough—for
corruptio optimi pessima—if the water filters through decayed
plants.

Whatever may be the basis for such beliefs, we see on
Dartmoor the meeting of the inviolate granite of the peaks
with crumbled strata; and round about this junction cliffs
as steep as on the seaside may be formed. The glory of this
landscape, lying high up on the rivers but well below the
often gentle acclivity of the mountain tops, is the essence of
Dartmoor. Whether its tors are two thousand feet or more
above the sea matters little in comparison.

It has been said that the proper National Park for England, at least, and perhaps for Britain, is the coast. Some of the western headlands have a peculiar claim and might be so reserved. Of them all the most suitable is the coast of Pembrokeshire from St. Bride's Bay to Goodwick near Fishguard and perhaps from St. Bride's Bay to Dale Harbour with those marvellous islands off the coast: Ramsey, Skokholm, Skomer and Grassholm. The population is small, the cliffs and bays are incomparable; and wild creatures of some rarity abound. St. David's Head is more impressive than Land's End, and the little known cromlech within the promontory is not the only sign of the prehistory of the region. Seals abound in and about the caves. St. David's Head was famous in hawking days for the breed of peregrine falcons that was found there; and there still, the peregrines nest and the rare chough, with buzzard and raven, birds so splendid that they become almost as important as the landscape. The islands teem with breeding birds. Grassholm is one of the few breeding haunts of the gannet and their great wings are as white clouds in the sky as you approach. Ten thousand nest there, and below their nursery you may see a dozen seals and more playing together. The multitude of birds on Skomer and Skokholm is scarcely credible. The ground above the cliffs quakes over the tunnels driven by nesting pairs of sheerwater and puffin; and hundreds of stormy petrel shelter in the ruined walls built by forgotten farmers before bracken and rabbits and isolation drove them to the mainland. Round the lighthouses, on the mainland as on the rocks, the migrant birds swarm like moths on a summer night. The spacious

Plate 31. The cliffs of North Devon

marshes, especially the vast Dowrog under the lion couch-ant of the hills behind St. David's Head is of its sort unique. It would be a wicked thing if 'developers' and amateur shack-builders and longshore vagrants with firearms or egg collecters and litter louts were allowed to sully and destroy this paradise of cliff scenery and wild life. If there were no other way it is possible that the rather contrary ideals of accessibility and sanctuary might be reconciled to the salvation of the most glorious part of 'little England beyond Wales'.

All the west coast should be sacrosanct. The reason why none is so fit to be created a National Park as this part of Pembrokeshire is that the population is small, and estab-lished seaside resorts are separated by wide intervals. Out-side Wales some sort of supremacy may be claimed for Hartland in Devon, which takes every visitor captive. From cliffs above the lighthouse you may see Tintagel to the south; and to the north both Baggy and Morte Point. This is the view to express the romance of the coast. No single rock competes with the impregnable Tintagel from which King Arthur went out to the fatal battle of Bodmin Mere. Cornwall has a stark strength all its own. The vir-tues of Hartland are different, more Devonian, one may say perhaps more English, although Arthurian legend belongs chiefly to Cornwall. History supplants myth.

Deep and rich with trees is the straight valley that separates the lighthouse from Hartland itself. The abbey was built in a pleasant place, full of inland comfort. Hart-land Church with its immense tower, visible a score of miles out to sea, is sterner; and yet quite remote from Cornish grimness or a superstitious sense. The six lime trees, that make an avenue to the lych-gate, suggest the loveliest corner of Penshurst, in Kent. The village partakes of the nature of an inland village. You must go a mile or two beyond the church before you suspect that you are at the very centre of west coast scenery. Inland qualities persist in some measure up to the very edge of the cliffs. There is a cowhouse and an inn at the very extremity of the point. Yet the wonder of sea and rock is as stark as nature made it. The tip-tilted strata, the jagged inhospitable rocks, the savage beaches, and the tall cliffs are common to the coast; but nowhere else are these associated with a like hinterland. Behind the Sugar-loaf hill and just south of Hartland Quay is a picture of downland, of green ridge and green hollow, a picture of lakeland with a half-hidden burn, with a marsh bright with the flag iris, fragrant with mint, and where the burn approaches the shore a waterfall, where the dippers play and the cry of oyster-catchers comes from the rocks below.

In many parts of Britain we are surprised to find a certain natural loneliness and wildness accompanied by relic signs of a busy civilisation in a previous age. Cromlech, barrow, cairn, road and camp survive in regions from which the population has long ago fled to warmer nooks and well watered valleys. Cornwall is littered with legendary symbols. By contrast the ghosts of Hartland are not prehistoric, are not even ancient, though a certain number of such relics are to be found. Hartland was a flourishing borough and even boasted a harbour, almost the other day. The loneliness is a new thing; and you feel it, even as you look at the three hundred feet of unassailable cliff and the jagged rocks of the lower shore sheltering the unceasing surf.

What Hartland was Bideford and Instow and Barn-staple became. The estuaries pleased a later civilisation; and the Taw and the Torridge attracted population that the high rocks repelled. Even as a place of pilgrimage the most ori-ginal and irregular bridge at Bideford is preferred before Hartland Point. Charles Kingsley's popularity in America is in part the cause; and Amyas Leigh is held to be a more romantic character than the monks of Hartland Abbey. How many thousand people go down the wide steps that are the only road into Clovelly and do not extend their journey to Hartland, either the Quay or the lighthouse! The lighthouse is as unlike other places as everything else in Hartland. Its site looks from above to be almost on the base of the rocks where they are washed by the sea; but the cliffs are big enough to destroy our common sense of perspective. They rise here and there to 350 feet; and this lowly perched lighthouse, away down there, is still more than a hundred feet above high tide level.

The walks along most of the Devon and north Cornish coast are convenient as well as magnificent; and the longest stretch is round Hartland to Bude and thereafter to Tintagel and beyond it up to Newquay. Round Hartland and round St. David's Head, and in some measure round Land's End and the Lizard, the coast keeps much of its wild grandeur.

Over the whole of the East of England and Wales the greater part of the most splendid scenes has been 'humanised' almost out of recognition though not out of beauty. The most notorious example is Blackpool. Compare, for example, Blackpool in Devon with Blackpool in Lancashire; and after Blackpool, Morecambe. By way of compensation the natural beauty of the hinterland is great, and it is often best seen from the neighbourhood of the shore. How full of colour is 'the Cambrian dome' of the Lakes seen from the broad sands of Morecambe Bay. The serene estuary of the Lune is backed by hills as masterful. Ingleborough Hill perhaps attracts more eyes than any hill within Britain, except the Peak of Derbyshire. A journey southward down the coast will disclose no such juxtaposition of a great population, whether in working or in holiday time, with a landscape so primal: immediately to the south the promon-tory of Heysham has become a great railway terminus and a port. The flat plain between Lune and Ribble is only less highly populated with small-holders and their poultry as Blackpool with holiday makers. Liverpool has done some-thing to save the Dee and the Wirral Peninsula from over-population. After all, Chester itself was the first harbour in the region, as the old water-tower announces, before it was supplanted first by Parkgate and then by Liverpool. When we pass from Cheshire into Flint we approach a succession of coastal resorts too fair not to be overwhelmingly popular for themselves alone. Further south again—from the vale of Clwyd and yet more emphatically as you approach Car-narvon—the shore seems to lean on the great mountains behind it; and the view up the river valleys is framed by high and shapely peaks. To the north of Blackpool the stone of the cliffs varies abruptly. The Great Orme's Head owes its prominence and colour to limestone alone. It is of a

piece, like a great statue carved to that particular end; and it
gives Llandudno a supreme quality among holiday resorts.
It has been more fortunate than the next great headland to
the south which, like some of the hillsides of Llanberis, has
been quarried to death. The mouth of the Conway rivals
the Dart in scenic quality and perhaps no building in the
island more fitly enhances the romance of its environment
than Conway Castle, and indeed the walls of the town
itself.

One of the surprises of travel is to cross the Menai Straits,
which are themselves unique, and to drive into Anglesey.
It is a pleasant isle, but almost humdrum, at least in conformation. If you have reached it from the region of Snowdonia, and past the grandeur of Carnarvon Castle, you feel
the force of anticlimax could no further go, though the fine
block of Holyhead itself restores the sense of Wales.

A little further south the coast is quite dominated by the
hinterland: the Roman Steps and the lake matter more to the
visitor than his seaside resort. In like manner many miles
further south does Cader Idris and the wild rocks about it
dominate such seaside townships as Pwllheli. Even the sea
birds find the hills irresistible; and one of the least approach-
able is known as the roosting place of the cormorants. No
man has played us more fantastic tricks with scenery than
the builder of the half-Italian village, in the corner made
by the oddly angled peninsula of Carnarvonshire. It is a
hilarious freak, carried out with the ingenuity of an architectural genius; and who will claim that it is an unsuccessful freak? The ardent preserver of Welsh scenery who
designed it knew his own region.

Merion lies in a corner of Cardigan Bay of which the best view is from Harlech Castle, perched on a very precipitous rock over the very flat plain that separates it from the sea. The site is supreme. And so we come to Barmouth and Dolgelly. Here, as at Aberystwyth further south again, the shore is everywhere backed by a magnificence of landscape, which even the mining of slate cannot wholly spoil.

The south coast of England comes between west and east in character as in place. When you move eastward from the Lizard almost all the coast is in some measure hospitable: and only here and there does the inland background concern either mariner or seaside visitor. Start Point is almost the most famous of landfalls. It announces the near neighbourhood of a close succession of harbours and anchorages of singular value and individuality. It would be a national sin to allow any part of such a friendly coast to be made either ugly or difficult of approach. Yet hideous houses appear close up against the cliff from Looe onwards, some denying the coast route to pedestrians. One of the most pleasant seaside walks in Britain, from the neighbourhood of Start Point to Salcombe, is likely to be disturbed, perhaps necessarily, by a wireless station. It was chosen for the sake of Cornwall, which had shown itself inhospitable to wireless waves. Between the harbours and pleasant seaside places of south-east Cornwall and Devon is one stretch quite forbidden to pedestrians. The shingle of the Chesil beach laid down and sorted out by the currents of the Channel is a unique thing and behind it here and there are lagoons that are neither broads nor lakes. Abbotsford is the supreme example. The stream checked by the bank of

stones spreads out into a brackish sheet of water enclosed
between the bank and great beds of reeds. It has been the
nursery of a thousand swans from a date earlier than the
building of the abbey. The wide duck decoy, shaped like a
starfish, in the inner pool is perhaps as old. The whole
scene is unforgettable. The swans themselves are hardly less
important to the scenery than the ten thousand gannets of
Grassholm. The great water dropwort in the ditches is
almost tree-like, and beyond the reeds and the lagoon the
huge bank of shingle rises like a mountain ridge and the
distant murmur of the waves seems out of place.

The shingle ends by Portland Bill where a very different
stone prevails. Is any stone so eloquent of its own history?
The sea shells of which it is chiefly composed are often so
well preserved by their matrix that the fluting of some of the
biggest is as perfect almost as it was before the inmates died,
those aeons ago. Architecturally, this stone is said to have
been discovered by Wren when seeking the best material
for St. Paul's.

The variety of the south coast between the granite of
Cornwall and the chalk of Hampshire lies in its colour as
well as conformation. The cliffs by Teignmouth are red with
soft sandstone. A little later the tint is a grey-blue where
the blue lias with its ammonites and other fossils emerges.
The other extremity of the narrow band is at Whitby. The
incomparable shape of Lulworth Cove, east of Weymouth
harbour, with its caves and recesses is due to the hammering
of the sea on the belted strata of limestone. Presently there
are no cliffs at all. It was on the flat land of Poole harbour
that first appeared the Spartina grass which has since been

used to reclaim the marshes of East Anglia. The Isle of Wight announces the chalk, queerly carved into pinnacles at the Needles and shaped into solid and pleasant curves in the Sussex cliffs known as the Five Sisters.

Beachy Head where the South Downs culminate is not less magnificent than the stubborn cliffs of the west. It is scarcely credible that so soft a material can raise so stiff a barrier against the waves and keep so precipitous a form. Yet five hundred feet of it butt into the Channel; and by height and salience surpass the greatest of the granite or limestone or old red sandstone cliffs. Eastbourne boasts as marvellous a cliff as St. David's or Hartland or Tintagel. The height seems to impress even the ribald jackdaws that tunnel nesting holes in the face. They seldom drop the lumps of chalk that they extract down that dizzy height, but fly with them to the top and place them sometimes in careful lines, along the grass edge.

Soon after the chalk begins to disappear; and there is a tendency—most concretely expressed at Rye—for the land to encroach on the sea. The last of the Cinque Ports are ports no longer. At Dungeness the sharp angle is made to jut further and further out by aid of the same force of wind and tide as piles up the Chesil beach. And so we come again to Walmer, where Caesar landed and to the christening cliffs of Albion by Dover harbour.

This coast is the greatest of all national possessions; and its preservation a great national duty. Some of it is past preservation. There are thirty miles in the south along which houses are virtually continuous. Littlehampton, Worthing, Lancing, Shoreham, Brighton, Rottingdean,

Peacehaven, Seaford and Newhaven are close neighbours, and of these Peacehaven and, in a very different way, Seaford are examples of most unhappy planning. Townships are nearly as contiguous from Christchurch to Poole or, on the west coast from Prestatyn to Rhyl and Llandudno. That glorious part of the east coast south of Berwick is threatened at a number of spots by shacks and ill-designed houses, not least in the neighbourhood of the pleasant bay and old town of Alnmouth. There will soon be no coast unsullied, if a wide and drastic planning scheme is not put into operation. We must plan the English scene or lose it. Since it must be human, let it be consonant with the humanities.

PRINTED IN GREAT BRITAIN
BY ROBERT MACLEHOSE AND CO. LTD.
THE UNIVERSITY PRESS, GLASGOW